ᚠ | Ansuz holds the power of the Æsir.

ᚦ | Thurisaz represents the power of Thor, a sign of protection but also represents the entities from Jǫtunheimr, allowing balance in our lives.

ᛟ | Othala is the rune of inheritance.

ᚷ | Gebo represents the gift of the gods. My gift to you.

Norse Gods and Goddesses

Guide to understanding Scandinavian Deities and the Viking Religion.

Ingvar Áskelson.

NeoViking Co.

Distribution by Lulu Press Self-Publishing Company.

Printed in the United States of America.

Ingvar Áskelson, NeoViking Co.

ISBN 978-0-6488855-0-4

To be kept up to date about future book publications and or Norse product releases, visit www.neotericviking.com and make your way to the bottom of the page. Alternatively, connect with me on Instagram @NeotericViking.

To the Norse Pagan community of the internet,

Thank you for making this possible.

Contents

PREFACE 1

ÆSIR 4

Óðinn

Frigg

Þórr

Baldr

Höðr

Viðar

Vali

Týr

Heimdallr

Bragi

Iðunn

Loki

Ull

Forseti

Mimir

Hœnir

Gefjon

Vár

Fulla

VANIR 71

Gullveig

Njörðr

Skaði

Yngvi

Freyja

JǪTNAR 83

Ægir

Rán

GLOSSARY OF TERMS 87

REFERENCE .... Error! Bookmark not defined.

I would firstly like to acknowledge a great educator in the field of Norse language and myth, Dr. Jackson Crawford. Thank you for your free-to-view YouTube videos and thank you to Stella for answering my emails.

Thank you to my good friend Taylor Jobling for reading and editing the content the first time around. I'd also like to express deep gratitude for my Nan who proof-read the content countless times.

I'd also like to acknowledge Brigón Munkholm and Adam Busch. Your descriptions and interpretations of the Norse Gods & Goddesses helped me greatly during the early stages of writing this book.

The mistakes within this book are attributable to me alone.

For business or general enquiries, email me here; Ingvar.NeotericViking@Gmail.Com

Sincerely,
Ingvar Áskelson.
11th February, 2021

Preface

In Norse society, 'fate' is referring to the unseeable forces of the infinite universe which, to an extent, is explained through metaphors in the Norse myths. Many have interpreted this to mean that your life events are fixed and you don't control what happens to you; I was one of those who believed it. But I have come to realize that isn't necessarily the truth. Future events are *not* fixed yet they *are* already determined. The Norse peoples understood that *our actions* of the past determine the parameters of present events, therefore heightening or lowering the likelihood of a potential event occurring in our lives. Multiple possible realities exist simultaneously. Our focus (*"hugr"*) and our actions determine which 'reality' becomes the experience of an individual. The Law of Attraction is always in play meaning that what you focus on will automatically be attracted to you, whether you want it or not. Whether the Norse peoples understood this specific concept is not made clear but it is evident that they were aware of the manipulation of energy within the universe and I believe this is an important concept for you to grasp, as it can be applied to your life.

It must also be made clear that there is no complete or comprehensive guide to the Norse Gods and Goddesses. This is because the ancient Scandinavian and Germanic people didn't write anything down, so it is impossible to know or understand what they understood. There are really only two groups of sources that help us understand the beliefs of pagan-Scandinavia; the Eddas and the Sagas of Viking heroes. The Poetic Edda is a compilation of orally composed poems (some dating to as early as 900) but transcribed at a later date (1200) and the Prose Edda is the work of an Icelandic-Christian poet attempting to preserve as much of pagan-Scandinavia as possible. Although, his attempt is to create a perfect hierarchical structure for a Christian audience, resulting in several interpretations being augmented. He was killed at the age of 62 in his own basement, in 1241. Skaldic poetry has served as a base in the preservation of the Norse Gods and Goddesses but like the other works, it was transcribed by writers who had already converted to Christianity and often misdirected readers and was even furthermore misinterpreted by those who read it without the proper context to kennings and such, leading to a mass spread of misinformation throughout the internet; I hope to reconcile this to the greatest extent possible.

The definitive line between *'god'* and *'human'* is very elusive but I would perceive a god as an entity who's conscious ability allows them to manipulate the environment around them against what is known as the scientific laws of humanity; therefore, performing something *'impossible'* and would appear as an entity with more *'power'* than a human. I consider all deities discussed within this book to be of a higher consciousness than humans, so all included in this list will be discussed in the context of a *'god.'*

This book is set within the *Norse cosmos.*

All Gods are descended from *Búri,* Oðinn's grandfather.

All Jötnar (giants) and Dvergr (dwarves) are descended from *Ymir*, the first being to exist.

The Jötnar are not physically larger than the gods, they are just a rivalling species who possess the same conscious abilities as the gods (perceived as magic).

The Æsir and Vanir were at war until it was decided that neither side could beat the other and they made a peace treaty through a hostage exchange.

All runes used are in Elder Futhark, as these are the runes that Óðinn gave to us.

All pronunciations are in reconstructed Old-Norse. (r) symbolizes a rolled r.

Although the primary sources we have access to are limited, I did my best to create a fulfilling guide for modern readers while maintaining authenticity to the true sources and the old ways. Because there aren't many conclusions, that gives you the freedom to make your own opinions. The gods live within us. Just remember that whoever you perceive our creator to be, we all are one and belong to the same source. Odin and the others can be perceived in many ways, so can the people in our lives... The Old Gods can help us understand ourselves and those around us. Please proceed with an open-mind, I hope this resonates with you and you can benefit from it.

If you want to further incorporate the Norse Gods and Norse culture into your daily life, you can follow me on Instagram for posts and updates @NeotericViking.

Skål my friends.

ÆSIR

ᚢᛗᛁᛏ
Óðinn
(Oh-thinn)

ANSUZ

Óðinn (meaning "the mad one." 'Oðr' meaning passionate or ecstatic and 'inn' being a possessive suffix) is the son of Bórr and Bestla and one of the oldest gods within the Norse cosmos. He had many years to develop his skills, such as rune casting, poetry and war strategy, and he governs all things great and small. He has built an empire for his family to live; this place is called Ásgarðr, and Óðinn's family is referred to as the Æsir. Óðinn is the husband of Frigg, and together they raised two sons, Baldr and Höðr. With the giantess Jörð, Óðinn fathered Thor. With the giantess Griðr, he fathered Viðar, and by the giantess Rindr, he fathered Vali.

Óðinn is the grandson of the first man to exist, so he was one of the very few beings in existence at the beginning of the universe. Although the Jötnar also existed at that time, they were not the desired ally for the gods. Óðinn and his brothers, Vili and Vé, had a bigger vision than what currently existed. So, they killed the first hrimÞurs ("frost-giant"), Ymir, and utilize its corpse to create the framework of a new living place: Miðgarðr (meaning "middle enclosure"). In doing so, they wiped out all the Jötnar, except one named Bergelmir, who escaped on a boat with his wife (this detail is only preserved through Snorri; therefore, it may be an attempt to appeal to a Christian audience, painting a similar picture to Noah's ark). The triad of gods gave shape to the world and set the mechanisms for the realm to function (within the skull of Ymir, the sky). At each corner, they set four dwarves- Norðri, Vestri, Suðri and Austri- whose shoulders support Ymir's skull.

The gushing blood of Ymir created the oceans, and they used his flesh to make soil. His eyebrows became the walls of the enclosure, and his bones made mountains. They used fragments of his teeth to make rocks, and they used his brains to create clouds. This place was on a different plane of existence for a new race of beings: humans. This was a race the gods could teach, interact with and use to their benefit. In the middle enclosure, the elements from the surrounding realms could mingle and propel the universe into the ecstatic growth that Óðinn and his brothers desired.

As the divine triad explored the place they had created, they found a pair of tree trunks washed up on the beach; one was an ash and the other an elm tree, so they named the trees Ask (male) and Embla (female). Óðinn gave them spirit and önd (breath), known to the Hindus as *prana* and to the Chinese as *chi*. Vili gave them Óðr (inspired mental activity), and Vé gave them speech and human senses. They were the first humans to exist.

• † •

In Ásgarðr, Óðinn built himself many spectacular halls, such as Valhöll ('Val' meaning 'fallen' or 'slain' and 'höll' meaning hall. This is the hall of slain warriors. The English equivalent being 'Valhalla'), which can be found in the midst of the marvellous grove called Glasir, in the land called Gladsheim. He also built Valaskjalf, a place with a roof of pure silver where happy gods can live. This is where the high-seat, Hlidskjalf, is located. When Óðinn isn't travelling, he spends many hours a day in his throne. From that vantage point, he can see everything that happens within the cosmos. Only his wife Frigg is allowed to sit there.

Valhöll is the place where Óðinn's army lives. The warriors are called Einherjar ('ein' meaning 'one' and 'heri' meaning 'warrior.' A group of lone warriors) and they are the strongest men from Miðgarðr. You will know Valhöll when you see it, as it is roofed with golden shields and held up by spear shafts. The one named Bragi, the master of words, will play his golden harp with grace to stimulate the visitors into a positive state. In the evening, swords will be brought out that are so polished, they illuminate the entire hall, and there is fine chainmail to be found on the benches as a gift from Óðinn to his visitors. It has six hundred and forty doors that will fit eight hundred Einherjar through each on the day that Ragnarök comes (meaning that Óðinn's hall can house up to 512,000 warriors). A wolf hangs above the western door and an eagle above him. In the courtyard of Valhöll, there is a tree called Læraðr. A goat and a stag chew at its limbs. From the goat's udders flow bright mead that fills Valhöll's cups, and from the stag's horns, drops of water fall into the well Hvergelmir, the place where all rivers originate.

In the morning, the Einherjar are awoken by a rooster called Gullinkambi (meaning "Golden-comb"), and they practice fighting until the evening. Then the dead warriors will rise again and feast with Óðinn and Freyja in the dining area, Fólkvangr—the place where Freyja arranges the seats. The cook is named Andhrimnir, and he lets the pork from Saehrimnir cook in the cauldron Eldhrimnir. According to Óðinn, there is no better meat than what the Einherjar eat.

Óðinn fears only a few things: Loki's mutant wolf-child and losing his ecstatic mental-inspiration, which is personified by his ravens, Huginn and Munin (meaning 'Thought' and 'Memory'). Loki's children, Fenrir, Jörmungandr and Hel were taken from their home in Jǫtunheimr at a young age by Thor and Tyr (at Óðinn's request) because Óðinn believed evil was to come of them. The bold gods brought the supernatural children to Óðinn, who was so fearful of the wolf's strength that he decided to permanently bind it. Óðinn was told by a Völva (Norse witch who practices the magic Seiðr) that Loki's son will break its bonds at

Ragnarök and devour him. In preparation, Óðinn assembles the largest army in the cosmos.

To build and strengthen his army, he contracts the Valkyries to reap the souls of men who fall in battle. The Valkyries have a mysterious nature about them and it seems that much information has been lost but from what we have, they are presumed to be mortal women with powers given by Óðinn. In Miðgarðr, there is a holy gate called Valgrind, which, considering the linguistics, can only be assumed to be is a gateway to Gladsheim, so the Valkyries can transport the souls of men to Valhöll. Six Valkyries are listed in the poem *Voluspá*. They are named Skuld, Skogul, Gunn, Hild, Gondul and Geirskogul. In the poem *Grimnismál*, St. 36, Óðinn lists thirteen Valkyries who live in Valhöll and bring the Einherjar beer.

"They bring my horn, my Valkyries! Hrist and Mist, Skeggjold and Skogul, Hild and Thruth, Hlokk and Herfjot, Goll and Geirolul, Randgrith, Rathgrith, and Reginleif- they bring the Einherjar beer."

> Óðinn's Valkyries Gunn, Rota and Skuld always ride to choose who shall be slain, and to govern the killings.

While in disguise, Óðinn deceives the kings of men and initiates wars between them. He uses fate runes to make the stronger side lose, so the superior warriors can be harvested and join his army in Valhöll. In the *Saga of the Volsungs*, the Valkyrie Brynhild is stung with a *svefnÞorn* ("sleep-thorn") for killing the wrong king during a battle. Here, Óðinn's power over others is demonstrated and it shows that he will use everything he can, to fight the inevitability of death.

• † •

After the first war, when the Æsir and Vanir tribes made peace, the gods collectively spat into a massive cauldron and derived a being from the mixture; his name was Kvasir. He was so wise that there was no question he couldn't provide a suitable answer to. Because of this gift, he wandered the realms, dispensing his wisdom and answering the questions of those he met. He followed that path until he ran into two dwarves named Fjalarr and Galarr (meaning 'deceiver' and 'screamer'), who killed him and drained his blood.

They mixed his blood with honey to create the mead of poetry, which they poured into three containers: two vats called Sodn and Bodn and a pot called Óðrerir, which the mead would assume the name of. Following the creation of Óðrerir, a Jötun named Gilling and his wife visited the dwarves. In short, Fjalarr and Galarr killed them both, which resulted in their son, Suttangr, coming to the dwelling of the dwarves and torturing them. He put them on a small, rocky reef-island below sea level until they begged for their lives. Suttangr took the mead of poetry and then stored the three containers in a mountain called Hnitbjörg under the protection of his daughter, Gunnloð.

Either because Kvasir didn't return to Ásgarðr for an extended period of time, or because Óðinn saw the events from his throne, he desired the mead of poetry. He travelled to Jǫtunheimr under the name Bǫlverkr (literally "evil-doer") and came by a group of nine workers, mowing a field with scythes. Bǫlverkr had a brilliant whetstone in his pocket, which he used to sharpen their scythes. The workers were all so impressed that they wondered what he would trade for the stone. Bǫlverkr said the last man standing could have it, after which he threw the whetstone into the air, watched the workers kill each other, caught the stone and carried on his way.

Bǫlverkr came to the house of the brother of Suttangr, Baugi. He announced that Baugi had lost nine workers in the field and suggested that he would do the work of nine men for the summer, under the condition that Baugi would help him secure a drink of the mead of poetry. Baugi agreed to the terms, and Óðinn did the work of nine men for the summer.

After that, Baugi went to his brother and asked if he would share any of the mead with his new farmhand, but Suttangr refused to give a drop away. Upon hearing that, Óðinn came up with another plan. He got out a drill known as Rati and instructed Baugi to bore into the mountain, Hnitbjörg. When Baugi said the deed was done, Óðinn blew into the hole but bits of rock flew back at him; he realized then that Baugi was trying to betray him. He told Baugi to keep drilling, and once the chamber was visible, Óðinn turned himself into a snake and slithered through the hole as Baugi tried to stab him.

When Óðinn made his way into the chamber (probably disguising himself as a more handsome man), he seduced Gunnloð and she agreed to give him three drinks of the mead in exchange for spending three nights with her. On the third night, Óðinn took his three drinks of mead and on each drink, he consumed an entire container. Óðinn then turned himself into an eagle and flew out of the mountain, headed back to Ásgarðr.

As Óðinn flew through the air, he didn't realise Suttangr had also turned into an eagle and was close behind him. When Oðinn looked back, he was so startled that he defecated some of the mead into Suttangr's face; that portion of mead is for bad poets. When Óðinn returned to Ásgarðr, he regurgitated the rest of the mead into a large cauldron, and it was then shared it with gods and humans.

In the poem *Hávamál*, Suttangr came to Ásgarðr searching for a man named Bǫlverkr, to which Óðinn responds, "Well, he's not here." Óðinn follows up with the famous St.110 of *Hávamál*,

"I believe that Óðinn swore an oath to them- but who can trust Óðinn? He left Suttangr deceived in his own home, and he left Gunnloð weeping."

• † •

Oðinn can be seen wearing a blue or grey cloak to cover his strong but aged body, wearing a golden arm-ring and wielding a spear. He chooses to wear a wide brimmed hat to cover his long grey hair which, in turn covers his missing right eye. He is always working with the runes and his ravens, who perch on his shoulders. Óðinn's command over language exceeds almost all others which leaves him sounding witty but in truth, he was likely deceiving you.

Óðinn is undoubtably a fan of all weapons but he will choose the spear before any other. He possesses a sacred spear called Gungnir, which was specially forged for him by the famous dwarf craftsmen, the sons of Ivaldi. His spear is carved with intricate runes that ensure any oath taken upon the spear cannot be broken. Gungnir will never miss its target, which is handy considering Óðinn's one-eyed-ness and his aim can be less than perfect. Óðinn also has a divine piece of armoured jewellery, an arm-ring called Draupnir. This ring multiplies every ninth night, into eight new arm-rings the same size and weight as the original. The rings can be used as a reward, a symbol or he can use them to increase his wealth.

Óðinn has two ravens named Huginn and Munin, whose names translate in the same way as Óðinn's name. *Hugr* meaning "thought," which is followed by the possessive suffix '*inn.*' It is the same with Munin, who is the personification of Óðinn's "memory." Due to Óðinn's ecstatic mental inspiration, his thought and memory cannot be contained within his physical body, so it travels within the projected energy field of Óðinn's entity (which can be assumed to be quite large). At dawn, Óðinn's ravens fly through the realms and gather information. At the last meal of the day, they return to Óðinn's shoulders and tell him of the news they discovered. He also has two wolves named Geri and Freki, meaning "greedy" and "ravenous." Óðinn feeds them his personal servings of meat because he can sustain his physical body on wine alone. His battle steed is called Sleipnir and it was born when Loki shapeshifted into a mare and seduced the stallion, Svaðilfóri. Loki gave birth to the eight-legged horse and Óðinn took it for himself. he says it is the greatest of all horses as Sleipnir can run over sky or sea, much faster than any other horse.

• † •

Óðinn has made many great sacrifices in his time, to fulfil his high ambitions and thirst for knowledge. Such as when he carved out his own eye and traded it to the beheaded god Mimir, for a drink of the wisdom-giving-waters found in Mimisbrunnr (meaning "Mimir's well"), which is located under the third root of Yggdrasil. Óðinn also hanged himself from an ash tree to learn the art of rune casting. Stanza 138 reads;

"I know that I hung on a wind battered tree, nine long nights, pierced by a spear and given to Óðinn, myself to myself, on that tree whose roots grow in a place no one has ever seen."

139; *"No one gave me food, no one gave me drink. At the end I peered down, I took the runes- screaming, I took them- and then I fell."*

He hung for nine days and nine nights, wounded by a spear, on what can only be assumed to be the world tree, the cosmic axis, Yggdrasil (pronounced; "Igg-drah-sill"). The poetic stanzas have been provided in raw form to allow you your own interpretation but mine lead me to believe that Óðinn teetered between life and death, in an effort to leave his physical body and connected with a higher consciousness, like many shamans around the world have been known to do, and was then able to interpret the runes. Old Norse to English translations will differ depending on the translator but you will consistently find these words;

"myself to myself."

Did Óðinn sacrifice the 'self', or ego, which had accumulated over his life in the physical form of 'Óðinn'? Surrendering and sacrificing the ego-self to a different 'self.' A higher-self which possessed greater spiritual knowledge and was therefore able to teach the runes to the ego-self.

The two stanzas above are the *only* mention of this incident of 'self-sacrifice,' other than the following stanzas 140, and 141 which further elaborate on the spells Óðinn was able to learn and how his mind expanded to the point where he could hardly control the words coming from his mouth or the deeds being done by his hands.

There is no hard evidence within the Eddas as to whether there is an even higher dimensional plane above that of the gods but in the Prose Edda, the one disguised as *High'* (assumedly Óðinn, Tyr or Heimdallr) said to Danish king Gylfi,

"They say there is another heaven south of and above this heaven of ours, and that heaven is called Andlang; and that there is a third heaven still further above that one, and that is called Vidblain, and it is in that heaven that we believe this place to be. But we believe it is only light-elves that inhabit these places for the time being."

Putting aside that this was transcribed by a Christian poet, it opens the question; what did the ancient Germanic and Scandinavian people know about dimensional travel? This is a distinct mention of two additional dimensions above and beyond that which the Northern Mythology covers and it says that only beings of light inhabit those places.

Considering Óðinn's age, it shouldn't come as a surprise that he is travelling constantly. His expeditions even last for years at a time, seeking the answers to his unending questions. In the poem *Voluspá*, Óðinn resurrects a dead Völva, a Norse witch who practices Seiðr magic and is able to make prophecies. She rose from her grave and Óðinn made her explain the beginning and end of the world to him. Another example of this is when Óðinn travelled to the realm of the dead and committed the same act but achieved the knowledge of why his son was having visions of death.

Whenever Óðinn travels, he is always in disguise. As such, he goes by many names, such as *Shadowed-Face*, *Hel-blind*, *Grey-beard* and *Good Advisor*. There have been over one-hundred names recorded that Óðinn has used to travel under. He spent many years disguised as a witch, living among humans, and he disguised himself as a ferryman to deceive his own son. Óðinn goes by many names and many faces; he deceives many with his spell-casting ability. Óðinn loves to fight and is fascinated by weapons but most importantly, Óðinn does everything within his power to prevent the death of his family.

ᚹRIX
Frigg
(F(r)-igg)

FEHU

Frigg (deeply rooted to the Proto-Germanic word 'Frijjō', meaning; 'the loving of one') is the wife of Oðinn and queen of the Æsir; she is highest ranking of the Ásyniur. According to Snorri, Saga is second and she rules the hall Sokkvabekk, which is a big place. Frigg is a loving mother to her sons Baldr and Höðr, and she often sits in Oðinn's throne, Hlidskjalf, to watch over the realms. She can be moody because Oðinn travels for such extended periods of time and shows little affection for her. She spends her days ensuring Ásgarðr is functioning to its full capacity and attending to those in need. Frigg's hall is located in the marshlands of Ásgarðr; it is called Fensalir.

It is common knowledge among the Æsir that Frigg knows the fates of all living beings, but she keeps them in confidence; like some of the other goddesses. This is a characteristic found among the Norns, the choosers of fate. In the poem *Fafnismál*, St.13, it is stated by the dragon Fafnir that,

"There are various different kinds of Norns: they are not all of one family. Some are god-born, some are elves, others come from the dwarves."

It is evident that the Norns are of a diverse parentage and do not necessarily have a common ancestry. Good Norns are ones of noble parentage; they shape good lives, but evil Norns are responsible for the victims of misfortune. Although this is purely speculation and never explicitly stated, it is possible that Frigg is (*or was*) a Norn of the Æsir and spent her youthful years weaving the fates of gods and humans. This speculation is backed up by the fact that reference is always made to a magical string that is used to weave the fates into existence. And Frigg is supposedly the one who 'crafts' it. In the poem *Voluspá*, St.20, it states,

"Three wise women live there, by that well under that tree. Urðr is named one, another is Verðandi, the third is named Skuld. They carve men's fates, they determine destiny's laws, they choose the lifespan of every human child, and how each life will end."

The Norns mentioned in Voluspá reside under the first root of the tree Yggdrasil, by a very holy well which can be referred to as Urðr's well or the Well of Wyrd. According to Snorri, the Norns are not of equal age; he claims that Skuld is the youngest of them. The Norns take water from Urðr's well and mix it with the white mud that lies round the well. Then they pour the compound onto the roots of Yggdrasil to prevent rot and to combat the serpents who dwell beneath the second root that reaches down to Niflheimr. More snakes lie beneath the ash tree than anyone can comprehend. Yggdrasil suffers more than any person can contemplate; stags chew its leaves from the top, rot attacks from the side and Niðhoggr, that foul beast, eats away at the roots.

Frigg will often fly over the realms with her falcon suit in search of Oðinn. This is evident from the kenning frequently used to describe her: "queen of the falcon-suit." Due to her husband's relentless search for knowledge and travelling schedule, she feels lonely and unappreciated. She mothered two sons, Baldr and Höðr, but they are now grown, and she no longer feels like she is needed. This would explain why she chose to have her hall built in the marshlands of Ásgarðr; so she could care for the poor animals who live in the harsh environment.

In the poem *Lokasenna*, Loki claims that Frigg was lustful toward Oðinn's brothers Vili and Vé, which shows that the gods and goddesses aren't perfect, divine creatures. The line between *god* and *human* is considerably thin as the powers of a god only appear to be extreme control of the will, which therefore can be used to manipulate the energy and matter around them. They are almost identical to humans and emotions can easily influence their actions.

• † •

Frigg knew the fate of her son Baldr; that he would be killed and taken to Hel, the realm of the dead, away from his family. Although Hel is often portrayed as an undesirable place, it is in fact a very pleasant afterlife for most. Frigg spoke forth her prophecy, that her son would be safe, then she travelled through all the realms and made all things pledge an oath never to harm her son. She spoke to fire, and it promised it would not burn him; water gave its oath never to drown him; iron would not cut him, nor would any of the other metals. Stones promised never to bruise his skin. Frigg spoke to trees; she conjured diseases and spoke to them, and all diseases that could hurt or wound a person agreed never to touch Baldr.

Frigg didn't pass by a single thing without making it swear its pledge to her son, except the plant mistletoe. When she passed by the oak trees, west of Valhöll, she saw the weed growing but thought that it was too small, young and insignificant to hurt Baldr. She returned to Ásgarðr with the news and shared, "Baldr is safe." The Æsir didn't believe her, so they made a circle around Baldr. They hacked at Baldr with axes, swords and spears but they touched his skin like feathers. Arrows would not pierce his skin and stones would whip past him.

Everyone laughed and cheered; enjoying the moment. Except Loki. Loki didn't smile. Loki didn't laugh. He slipped away during the commotion and constructed a plan to eliminate Baldr. Loki approached Frigg, disguised as the handmaiden Fulla, who shares Frigg's secrets. He questioned Frigg as to whether anything refused to pledge its vow to Baldr. She explained about how she examined then passed by the mistletoe. With this new information, Loki went to the oak trees west of Valhöll and saw the plants growing out of the bark. He saw the berries and thought about poisoning Baldr but he had something much more sinister in mind. Loki took the leaves and crafted a spear with a mistletoe tip. He gave it to Baldr's blind brother, Höðr. Höðr was so excited that he could finally participate in the fun event. So excited that he didn't think. Loki said he would guide Höðr's hand and told him to throw the spear as hard as he could. Höðr threw the spear at his brother, and all the gods stopped laughing. The gods stopped cheering. Because Baldr was dead; this was Frigg's first sorrow.

ÞꝊR
Þórr
T-o(rr))

THURISAZ

Thor (meaning; "thunder") is a hard worker who would rather spend his time getting business done than drinking and partying with the other gods, although he loves drinking and partying too. He works hard, he plays hard and he parties hard. He is the greatest drinking man in all the cosmos, which will be elaborated on later. Thor is the first son of Oðinn, and his mother is the giantess Jörð (meaning "Earth"). Thor's life is dedicated to protecting Miðgarðr (middle-enclosure, Earth, his mother) and keeping humans safe from the evil forces that come out of Jǫtunheimr.

Since boyhood, his physical size and strength have been unmatched. Oðinn raised Thor into the god he is today, and now, he is the most famous man in Scandinavia (considering the number of place-names in comparison to any other god or goddess). Thor can be joked with on occasion, but he has a scarily short temper. He will often spend his days east of Ásgarðr, in Jǫtunheimr, clearing the lands of as many Jötnar as he can. It works two ways; as stress relief and eliminating the enemy of gods and humans. Apparently, Scandinavia was polluted with Jötnar until Thor cleared it for us to live safely.

Thor has a land of his own that exists near Ásgarðr; it is called Thruðheimr (thru-th-hay-mer). In his realm, he has a massive hall that he built for himself. Oðinn admits that it is the largest of all roofed homes. It has five hundred and forty rooms and it is called Bilskirnir. Thor will awaken in his home with his beautiful family, Sif, Magni, Modi and Thrud.

His wife is the goddess Sif; she has the longest and most radiant golden hair in all the cosmos. Barely any other information of Sif has been preserved, but she is also the mother to the oath keeper of the gods, Ullr. Modi and Thrud were conceived by Thor and Sif, but Magni's mother is a Jötun woman named Járnsaxa.

Thor has long red hair and a thick red beard to compliment his incredibly muscular physique. Although his choice of word is basic, his fiery eyes and menacing appearance intimidate his enemies to the core. The bold god equips himself with a pair of iron gauntlets called Járngripr and a belt that doubles his strength, called Megingjörð. These are required to amass enough strength to wield the short-handled hammer, Mjölnir (pronounced; m-yoll-near).

His hammer is the most powerful weapon within the Norse cosmos and was crafted by the famous dwarf-blacksmith brothers, Brokkr and Eitri. It can destroy anything it touches and will return to Thor if he throws it. Mjölnir can also be shrunk down to the size of a pendant so Thor can disguise himself when travelling.

Thor rides across the sky on a chariot pulled by his two goats, Tanngrisnir and Tanngnjostr (meaning; "teeth-snarler" and "teeth-grinder"). Because of the sacred powers within Mjölnir, Thor can eat the meat off the bones of his goats, pile the bones and resurrect them again the following morning.

• † •

Thor is widespread known as the strongest man in the cosmos, but he was humiliated when he couldn't even lift the cat of the famous Jötun, Utgard-Loki (not to be confused with Loki). The story begins with Thor and Loki roaming through Jǫtunheimr with Thor's goats. The day was coming to a close and they stumbled upon a farm, so Thor and Loki approached the owner and asked to stay the night; the farmer obliged them as good hospitality is a key value of Norse society. Thor announced that they didn't come empty-handed; he had brought food for all to enjoy. He said they could eat his two goats but firmly established not to fracture the bones, only to pile them on top of the skins.

The farmer and his family ate the meat, alongside Thor and Loki, but the son of the farmer, Thjálfi, was tempted to break one of the leg bones and suck the marrow out. In the morning, Thor took Mjölnir in his hand and cast a spell over the goats, bringing them back to life; but one had a lame leg. Thor was infuriated and threatened to kill the whole family but the father said, "No, let's be reasonable. Instead, take my children as your slaves for life."

The children were named Thjálfi and Roskva, and Thor happily took them as his slaves. Thor and Loki continued on their way and found themselves at a small house in which they could stay the following night. In the morning, they were awoken by a loud voice. "I found my glove," said a truly giant man. Skrýmir was his name, and he was travelling in the same direction, so he offered to carry their provisions in his enormous bag.

They travelled for another day and set down for camp. Skrýmir was the first to sleep, so he said the other could open his bag and take what they needed. Thor tried to open it, but he wasn't strong enough to untie the knot. Obviously, this made Thor furious, so he rushed up to Skrýmir's head and slammed the crown of his head with Mjölnir. He felt the face of his hammer sink deep into Skrýmir's head. The giant woke up and said, "Did a leaf fall on my head? Is it time to wake up yet, Thor?" Thor said, "No, it was just a leaf or something; go back to sleep." So Skrýmir went back to sleep and Thor tried again. This time, he struck Skrýmir in the temple and sunk his hammer into the handle, but the giant remained asleep. On the third time, Skrýmir woke up and said it was close enough to dawn, so he got up.

At this point, Skrýmir informed them of the Jötun named Utgard-Loki, whose hall was located to the East. Skrýmir told them they were near the enormous home of Utgard-Loki but also provided a warning that he wouldn't think much of Thor and Loki considering they were so tiny in comparison. When they arrived, they had to bend their heads back to touch their spines before they could see over the top of the castle.

The gate was locked but Thor, Loki and the child slaves made their way through one of the gaps in the gate because they were so tiny. When they found Utgard-Loki, he said the travellers could stay the night if they were able to demonstrate some sort of exceptional talent. Loki was the first to speak up and was contested by Utgard-Loki's man, Logi, in an eating contest. Loki lost. Thjálfi said he was a fast runner, so he was paired against Utgard-Loki's child, Hugi. Thjálfi lost.

Utgard-Loki was disappointed, but he turned to Thor with hope. He said, "Thor, what can you do?" Thor announced that he was a great drykkjumaðr (meaning 'drinking-man'). Utgard-Loki provided him with a drinking horn filled with mead and said that any man in his company could drink its entirety in a single gulp. Some men might take two but no man was such a pathetic drinking man that he would need to take a third.

Thor turned the horn up, but by the time he required a breath, the level had barely dropped. He took a second gulp and not much had changed. On his third gulp of mead, the level had only dropped a thumb's width. Thor was disgusted and embarrassed with himself, so Utgard-Loki offered him another challenge to redeem himself. Thor said he was strong, but Utgard-Loki didn't think it would be fair for Thor to try and lift any of the men, so he offered for Thor to lift his grey cat (which wasn't very big on an Utgard-Loki scale). Thor got under the cat and heaved with all his strength but he couldn't lift more than a single paw off the ground. Utgard-Loki said, "Come on, Thor, just try to lift my cat."

Thor said, "Now I'm angry, so I will wrestle any of your men." Utgard-Loki said, "There isn't anyone in my company who would be a fair match, considering your size and obvious lack of strength. Thor, you can wrestle my grandmother, Elli." They wrestled for some time but Elli specialized in many forms of combat and forced Thor to tap out. Regardless, Utgard-Loki allowed them to stay the night for their considerable efforts.

In the morning, Utgard-Loki showed them out but made a confession to Thor. He said he was using magic to deceive them. Utgard-Loki admitted that *he was* the giant man Skrýmir, that he was using magic to appear so huge and he used magic to move hills in the way of Thor's hammer strikes. He said that valleys were made from Thor's hammer. Utgard-Loki also said that Loki's competitor, Logi, was none other than flame. Nothing can devour faster than flame. Thjálfi's competitor, Hugi, was nothing less than thought. Because no one can race faster than thought.

Utgard-Loki said that the drinking horn was actually attached to the ocean and if Thor went to the ocean's edge, he would see that the ocean level had dropped substantially. He also said that the grey cat was actually the Miðgarðsormr in disguise. Elli was actually old age and no one can fight old age, not even the gods. This made Thor even angrier but when he tried to hit Utgard-Loki with Mjölnir, Utgard-Loki used magic to disappear.

• † •

Thor has battled with many famous Jötnar in his time and always came out victorious. The story of when Thor fought Hrungnir begins with Oðinn in disguise. Oðinn rode to Jǫtunheimr on Sleipnir, claiming that his horse was faster than any other horse, after which, Hrungnir challenged Oðinn to a race. Oðinn easily outpaced the Jötun and led him straight through the gates of Ásgarðr. The goddesses brought out good food and mead for Hrungnir and provided them in the dishes that Thor would normally use. Hrungnir drained each of Thor's goblets and became so drunk that he threatened to kill all the gods, except for Freyja and Sif. He also said that he would drink all their mead and move Valhöll to Jǫtunheimr. At that point, the gods had enough and they signalled for Thor to return home.

When Thor returned, he came up behind Hrungnir and raised his hammer, prepared to kill him on the spot but the gods argued that Ásgarðr was too sacred to kill anyone and Hrungnir argued that Thor would be a coward for killing an unarmed man. They arranged a time in Jǫtunheimr to duel, at a place called Griotunagardar. This duel was particularly important, as no one had ever challenged Thor to single combat, and Hrungnir was the strongest of the Jötnar, so there was much riding on his victory.

Hrungnir was accompanied by a giant creature made of clay, named Mokkurkálfi. He was nine leagues tall but only possessed the heart of a mare. So, when Thor came into its view, Mokkurkálfi stood motionless, urinating on itself. Meanwhile, Thor's boy slave Thjálfi, approached Hrungnir and told him that Thor was going to tunnel underground and come from beneath him, so Hrungnir stood on his shield. Thor, in a powerful rage, raced toward Hrungnir and launched Mjölnir in his direction. Hrungnir threw his weapon of choice, a whetstone. The weapons collided mid-air, and the whetstone shattered but a fragment lodged into Thor's forehead. The remaining fragments of whetstone fell down to Miðgarðr and created all the whetstone rocks in the world. The sheer force of Mjölnir couldn't be stopped. It crashed into Hrungnir's head and the Jötun's skull shattered as well.

When the whetstone lodged in Thor's brow, he fell forward, as did Hrungnir, whose leg pinned Thor to the ground by the neck. All the

Æsir tried to lift it but Magni, Thor's boy, who was only three years of age, was the only one strong enough to lift the massive leg. He said,

"Isn't it a terrible shame, Father, that I arrived so late. I think I would have knocked this giant into Hel with my fist if I had come across him."

Thor hugged his son warmly and gave the golden-maned horse of Hrungnir, Gullfaxi, to his son, which Oðinn was very jealous of. When Thor returned home, the whetstone remained in his head, but a sorceress named Groa was summoned. She was the wife of Aurvandil the Bold, a friend of Thor. She chanted spells over Thor until the whetstone became loose. At this point, Thor believed it would be removed, so he described the way he would repay Groa. He told her of the tidings of which he waded through, south across Elivagar, carrying Aurvandil in a basket on his back. He said one of the toes of Aurvandil was sticking out and it became frozen, so Thor broke it off and threw it up into the sky, creating the star called *'Aurvandil's Toe.'* Thor said it wouldn't be long until Aurvandil was home; Groa was so pleased that she couldn't remember any of her spells. So, the stone remained in Thor's brow.

• † •

Another famous battle begins with Loki using Freyja's falcon suit to fly into Jǫtunheimr. Loki perched on the high windowsill of a giant named Geirroðr; whom he wished to inspect. Geirroðr was suspicious of the bird, so he sent a servant out to grab bird-Loki. The servant climbed the wall with great difficulty and it pleased Loki to see this cause them so much trouble. So, he delayed the flight until the man had performed the entirety of the difficult climb. But when he attempted to jump away, his feet were glued to the windowsill by magic. Upon looking into Loki's eyes, the Jötun believed it must be a person, so Geirroðr put bird-Loki into a treasure chest for a 3-month starvation period.

After the time had passed, Geirroðr said he would allow Loki to go free if he could convince Thor to travel into Jǫtunheimr without Mjölnir or his equipment. Loki managed to do this, and Thor went to Jǫtunheimr. He stayed with a giantess named Griðr, who is the mother of his (then unborn) stepbrother, Viðar. He stayed for a single night, and she provided him with a new set of iron gloves, a belt of strength and an iron staff to wield, which is known as *Griðr's Pole*.

Thor approached the river called Vimur and buckled on his new belt, as Loki held on underneath. When Thor reached the middle of the river, it washed up over his shoulders, and he found himself nearly drowning. He looked up stream and realised it was one of Geirroðr's daughters urinating the river, so Thor stated, "A river ought to be dammed at its source." He managed to pick up a large boulder and do exactly that. He pulled himself to shore with a rowan tree, which is responsible for the kennings *"Thor's salvation."*

Firstly, they were shown into a goat-shed where there was a single seat, which Thor sat on. After doing so, he found himself being lifted into the air, so he pushed against the rafters with the iron staff. He heard a loud crack accompanied by a great scream. The daughters Gjalp and Greip were now dead. Geirroðr called Thor into the hall for games; when Thor entered, Geirroðr used a pair of tongs to pick up a lump of hot iron and throw it at the bold god. With his new gauntlets, Thor caught the iron while Geirroðr took cover behind an iron pillar. Thor returned it so hard that it destroyed the pillar along with Geirroðr's skull.

• † •

On another day, when Thor awoke, he was angry. He searched all around Ásgarðr but his hammer was missing. He went straight to Loki. The first thing he said was,

"Listen to me, Loki, listen to this: something never known before, in Miðgarðr or in Ásgarðr, has happened: Mjölnir's been stolen!"

They went to Freyja's lovely home, and Loki asked to borrow her falcon suit. She replied,

"I would give it to you, even if it were made of gold; I would loan it to you, even if it were made of silver."

With possession of the falcon suit, Loki flew and his feathers whistled as he came into range of Jǫtunheimr. There, he saw Thrym, a king of giants sitting on a mound, fastening the golden chains on his dogs' necks. Thrym asked what the news was and why Loki had come to Jǫtunheimr alone. Loki explained and asked if Thrym knew anything of where Mjölnir was. Thrym said he hid Mjölnir eight miles below the earth, and no one would see it again unless Freyja was brought to him as his bride.

When Loki returned to Ásgarðr, Thor met him and said,

"Were your efforts rewarded on this journey? Stay in the air, and tell me what news you have. Stories are often forgotten when the teller sits down, and lies are often told when people lie down."

Loki said his efforts were rewarded and he explained the situation to Thor. Thor went to find Freyja, he said,

"Freyja, put on a wedding dress! The two of us, man and woman, are going to Jǫtunheimr."

Freyja snorted so hard that the homes of the gods shook and her necklace, Brisingamen, trembled on her neck. Soon, all the gods met for a conference and they spoke a long time about how to get Thor's hammer back. It was Heimdallr who said,

"Let's put a wedding dress on Thor! Let him wear Freyja's necklace, the Brisingamen."

Thor argued, but they all knew it was the best chance they had at getting Mjölnir back. Loki said,

"Silence, Thor! No more of that talk! Unless you can get your hammer back, the giants will soon live in Ásgarðr!"

So, they put a wedding dress on Thor, they put Brisingamen on his neck and put a chain of jingling keys at his belt; they placed jewels on his chest and wrapped a pretty headdress around his head.

Surprisingly, Loki happily volunteered to go with Thor as a willing aid in the mission to retrieve the stolen hammer, the most powerful weapon in the cosmos. As they rode into Jǫtunheimr, mountains crumbled and the ground burst into flames under Thor's chariot. When the pair arrived in Thrym's hall, he announced their presence and the food was brought out. All on his own, Thor ate a whole ox, eight salmon, all the delicacies reserved for the women and drank three kegs of mead. Fortunately, when Thrym questioned "Freyja's" behaviour, Loki strung his words together and deceived the giant into believing that "Freyja" had abstained from eating for nine nights.

Thrym's sister came in and thought she would claim the customary gift from the bride. She said,

"Give me some of your golden rings, if you want to win my love, my affection, and a good welcome from me."

Thor refused to provide any gifts until the holy hammer was brought out and laid upon his lap. Then he laughed with a full heart, gripped the handle and killed every giant in Thrym's hall. He crippled all the giant's kin and repaid Thrym's sister with a blow of his hammer instead of golden rings. This is the way Oðinn's son got his hammer back.

• † •

Thor has a long and complicated relationship with Loki's serpent son, Jörmungandr (simply meaning "big monster"). Thor was the one who captured and took Jörmungandr away from his home in Jǫtunheimr. He brought the mutant serpent to Oðinn, where he was thrown in the ocean for the remainder of his day. Understandably, Jörmungandr hated Thor for this. Thor's reciprocal hate for Jörmungandr came about when he was deceived into thinking he was lifting a cat, but in fact, he was trying to lift Jörmungandr and was humiliated in a hall full of Jötun.

The third time he came into contact with the Miðgarðsormr was during a fishing expedition with Tyr's Jötun father, Hymir. This story begins with a large feast in the hall of Ægir, a great friend of the gods. Every season, the gods would visit Ægir and have great parties, but the only problem was that there wasn't enough mead for all the gods to enjoy. This time around, Ægir asked Thor to find a cauldron large enough to brew beer for everyone. This was partially a way for Ægir to get back at Thor for talking to him in an aggressive and demeaning tone.

Tyr overheard the conversation and knew where to find one. He approached Thor in private and revealed that his wise father, Hymir, who lived near the edge of the sky, owned a cauldron that was a mile deep, so Thor and Tyr set off into Jǫtunheimr. When they arrived in Hymir's home, they were greeted by Tyr's nine-hundred-headed grandmother and his mother, who is described as being "all golden, with a pretty face."

When Hymir came home from a long fishing expedition, he was not happy to see the enemy of the giants standing in his living room. Still, Hymir provided good hospitality for Thor and his son, killing three of his own bulls to feed them. Thor happily ate two by himself.

Hymir said that they would need to go fishing if they wanted to eat the next day, so Thor decided to cut the head off of one of Hymir's bulls as bait. Thor volunteered to row, so he could direct the boat into the deep ocean; this is because he wanted to catch the Miðgarðsormr. Thor threw his baited line into the water, and the serpent came rearing from the depths. The bold god pulled the serpent aboard the boat and struck it furiously with his hammer. Jörmungandr howled so violently that volcanoes erupted and the earth trembled, but the monster sank back into the waves.

Hymir was gloomy after this; he didn't say a word until they got back to shore. Once they arrived, Hymir said Thor must do his half of the work by either carrying the whales he caught to the house or tying up the boat. Thor ignored the requests and decided to pick up the boat (with its oars and buckets) and carry it through the forest, to Hymir's home.

Hymir was even more angered by Thor's actions, so he told Thor that a truly strong man would be able to break his glass cup. Thor destroyed many things by throwing the cup at them, but the cup wouldn't break. This was until Tyr's mother told Thor that Hymir's head is stronger than any cup, so he hurled the cup at Hymir's head, and it shattered. Thor passed the test, so Hymir said they could take his cauldron.

Tyr tried to lift it, but it remained unmoved. Thor took a turn and his feet broke through the floor, but he managed to lift the cauldron over his head and carry it a fair way, until he realised Hymir was chasing them with an army of Jötnar. Thor put the cauldron down and killed all those giants, including Tyr's father. He carried the huge cauldron to Ægir's hall, and now the gods drink the best mead there every season.

Thor will meet Jörmungandr for the final time at Ragnarök. They will face off in single combat at the edge of the ocean. He will strike the serpent in the head, killing it this time but Thor will walk no more than nine paces before falling dead from its venom that it had sprayed over the beach. It is told that Thor's sons Magni and Modi will survive Ragnarök, inherit Mjölnir and inhabit the heavens with Oðinn's sons.

Thor will do whatever it takes to ensure the safety of humans and our planet, but it is stated in the poem *Voluspá*, St.24,

"All humankind will die out of the world when Thor falls."

ᛒᚠᛏᛗᚱ
Baldr
(Boll-de(rr))

WUNJO

Baldr (meaning; "warrior") is the shining son of Oðinn, the most loved and respected among the Æsir. His fairness and wisdom exceed all those around him and his energy vibrates so highly that light radiates from him. He is the most beautiful son; a brilliant warrior and the gods never wanted any harm to come of him. He is beautifully spoken and the most merciful among the Æsir. He is described as having hair and eyebrows as white as snow, meaning that it was blonde and very attractive.

Baldr is married to the goddess Nanna and together, they bore Forseti, the god who settles disputes. Nanna isn't commonly attested to in the surviving pre-Christian sources, but she is often referred to as the goddess of joy and love because her love toward her husband never wavers. They spend an extensive amount of time together in Baldr's celestial hall, Breiðablik. No unclean thing is allowed in Breiðablik. Oðinn says, "That's a place where I know you'll find little grief." Nanna's lineage is unknown and from what I know, she isn't referenced in any stories other than that of Baldr's death, where she throws herself onto the funeral pyre out of grief. She follows Baldr through life, death and rebirth into the new world (post Ragnarök).

• † •

In the poem *Baldrs Draumar*, Baldr is seeing visions of death in his sleep. The gods met at a Thing and discussed why Baldr was dreaming of death.

They couldn't come to a conclusion, so Oðinn put a saddle on Sleipnir and rode down to Hel, where he faced the dog of Hel, Garmr. It was restrained but had a bloody chest and barked a long time while Oðinn passed through. The stones of the road rattled as he rode to the high house of Hel, known as Eliudnir. It was a great mansion but Oðinn's interests were elsewhere; he travelled east until he found the grave of a witch. He spoke a spell and forced her corpse to rise.

Oðinn asked her to share the news of Hel and what is to be expected in the realm of Niflheimr. He wanted to know why the benches were covered in straw and the floors covered in gold. The Völva said mead was brewing and food was being prepared for the arrival of Baldr. The Seeress said that Höðr would bear a long spear, and he would steal the life of Baldr.

Following that, in St.11, the Völva says,

"In halls to the west, Rindr will give birth to your son Vali; he will avenge Baldr when he is only one night old. He will neither comb his hair nor wash his hands till he puts Baldr's killer on the funeral pyre."

When Oðinn returned to Ásgarðr, he told Frigg of the news and she immediately set out and made all things pledge an oath never to harm Baldr. When Baldr's loving mother returned to Ásgarðr, she announced, "Baldr is safe." The gods threw axes and spears at Baldr but nothing could injure him. They were all filled with joy at the sight of their favourite god, unable to be harmed. Everyone laughed. Except Loki. The gods were amused for some time, so during the commotion, Loki slipped away and began to plot against Baldr. Loki took the form of the handmaiden Fulla, a close friend of Frigg, and discussed with her about the oaths. Loki eventually manipulated Frigg into telling him that mistletoe never swore any oath of protection.

With this information, Loki crafted a spear with a mistletoe tip and gave it to Höðr, Baldr's blind brother. Höðr was so excited he was able to participate and have fun with all the other gods. Loki guided Höðr's hand and told him when to throw the spear. When it happened, the gods stopped laughing and cheering because Baldr was dead.

• † •

Baldr was given a great funeral, which many gods, elves and dwarves attended. He was laid on his massive ship called Hringhorni with large amounts of treasure to take with him to the afterlife. When Baldr was carried out, Nep's daughter, Nanna, collapsed in grief and was also put on the ship. The Æsir wanted to perform Baldr's funeral, but the ship refused to move. So, they sent for a giantess named Hyrökkin, who rode a wolf using vipers as reins. When she dismounted, four berserkers were required to restrain it.

Hyrökkin pushed the boat with her first touch, and this enraged Thor so much that he almost smashed her head in but the gods begged for grace. Before Oðinn's son was pushed out to sea, Oðinn boarded the ship, gave Baldr his sacred ring, Draupnir, and whispered something in his son's ear—something that no other man knows, except Oðinn himself; which he used to win his contest of knowledge with the Jötun Riddle-Weaver. Thor consecrated the pyre with Mjölnir and set the ship alight, when a dwarf named Litr ran in front of his foot and he launched it into the fire.

The gods were gloomy after that day. They all wept, and they all wanted Baldr back in their lives. Oðinn went into his massive hall, Valhöll, and asked for a volunteer to travel down to Hel to see if Baldr could be bargained out of the realm of the dead. A warrior named Hermöðr came forth to the gods and said he would travel to Hel. Oðinn gave this man his brilliant horse Sleipnir and Hermöðr rode from Ásgarðr to Hel; a journey which the horse was accustomed to. When Hermöðr arrived at the Gjöll bridge, it was covered in gold and there was a maiden named Modgud guarding it. He stated his mission and she said,

"Downwards and northwards lies the road to Hel."

When Hermöðr reached Hel's gates, Sleipnir jumped so hard that they didn't come close to the top of the gate. When he entered, he saw that there were comfortable straw chairs, mead brewing and a good feast; Baldr and Nanna were being taken care of.

The daughter of Loki, Hel, said,

"If everything in all the worlds will weep for Baldr, I will send him back to Ásgarðr."

Before Hermöðr left, Baldr gave Draupnir back as a keepsake and Nanna sent Frigg a linen robe with a few other gifts too, including a ring for Fulla. When the news reached Ásgarðr, messengers were immediately sent through all the realms to ask everything to weep for Baldr. And everything did. But on the way back to Ásgarðr, through Jǫtunheimr, they discovered a Jötun woman in a cave who had yet to weep for Baldr. She was named Thokk (meaning "thanks"). She said that Baldr never did anything for her, so she would not weep for him. This woman was really Loki in disguise.

Because of Loki, Baldr was killed and because of Loki, Baldr was kept in the realm of the dead until the passing of Ragnarök. Baldr will survive Ragnarök, alongside his brothers and the sons of Thor. In the poem *Voluspá*, St.60-61, it states,

"Baldr will come back. Höðr and Baldr will live in Oðinn's hall, as well as other gods. Then Hœnir will speak forth his prophecies, and the two sons of Oðinn, the two brothers, will inhabit the heavens."

ᚺᚬᚦᚱ
Höðr
(H-oh-ther)

Höðr (meaning; "warrior") is the blind son of Oðinn and Frigg. He is a bold warrior and so strong that the gods would prefer the Ás not mention the work of his hands as it will be kept in the minds of men and gods for a long time. He was born without sight, but not much else is known of him. Höðr killed his brother Baldr, by the trickery of Loki, and was executed for it. Although, both Baldr and Höðr survive to see days past Ragnarök.

ᛩᛁᛏᚠᚱ
Viðar
(Vee-thar)

Viðar (possible meaning; "silent one" or "wide ruler") is the silent son of Oðinn and Griðr; he is a source of great support to the gods in any kind of danger. As a child, Viðar would grow plants in his garden and wait, watching them grow. Oðinn says in *Grimnismál* that Viðar's wide land is now overgrown with grass and weeds. He spent a lot of time by himself because he needed time to prepare. He had the responsibility of killing Fenrir at Ragnarök. Viðar owns a powerful leather boot, which adopts all the leather scraps thrown away by humans. Giving your leather scraps to Viðar will assist him in opening Fenrir's mouth open and killing the enemy of the gods. At Ragnarök, Viðar will use his powerful boot to hold Fenrir's jaws apart and shove his sword into the mouth of the giant wolf. The blade will reach to his heart and kill him.

ᚹᚨᛚᛁ
Vali
(Voll-e)

Vali is the vengeful son of Oðinn. Vali was born by the Jötun woman, Rindr. After Baldr's death, Oðinn fled Ásgarðr and disguised himself as a woman to deceive the giantess. He told Rindr's father that he needed to chain her up in order to give her medicine. When Oðinn had the chance, he turned back into himself and proceeded to rape her. Vali was purely born to avenge the death of Baldr, for he was conceived and grew to manhood in a single night. Vali killed his half-brother that same day and killed Loki's son Narfi. Still, Vali is one of the few to survive Ragnarök. It is explicitly stated that Viðar and Vali will inhabit Gimle when Ragnarök has passed.

> *"Þá er Sloknar Sutrtalogi."*
>
> *"When Surtr's flame goes out."*

Some of the gods will return. The earth will rise a second time, out of the sea, green once again. Waterfalls will flow and eagles will fly overhead. Oðinn's sons Baldr, Höðr, Viðar and Vali, alongside Thor's sons, Magni and Modi, will make it past those dark days. The remainder of the Æsir will meet on Iðavöll, the place where their home once stood, and recall the great memories they once shared. They will find the golden game pieces of hnefatafl, which they once played with, scattered in the grass, as they make their new life at the mountain known as Gimle. It is a place more beautiful than light. Fields will bear harvest without labour, and all sickness will disappear. Hœnir, will speak his prophecies and the sons of Oðinn will inhabit the skies. Although not all is well, the foul dragon known as Niðhoggr will come flying from the dark mountains, bearing corpses in his wings.

ᛏᛁᛦ
Týr
(T-u(r))

TIWAZ

Tyr is a courageous man and powerful leader who loves a fight. His father is the giant Hymir and his mother is described as being "all golden with a pretty face." Although Tyr had no dwelling of his own in Ásgarðr, he was always welcomed to one of the golden seats in Valhöll, where the gods occasionally had meetings. There is very little evidence that demonstrates Tyr's qualities as a person, which is simply an issue of preservation. In the *Saga of the Volsungs*, the Valkyrie Brynhild says,

"You should carve victory-runes if you want to have victory. Carve some on the hilt of your sword, carve some on the middle of the blade also, some elsewhere on the sword, and name Tyr twice."

Evidently, Tyr has great power over victories in battle and will grant it to those who attempt to make contact with him with a great desire. According to Snorri, upon analysis of many poems, those who are known as "ty-valiant" will surpass any other man in courage and non-hesitance. Tyr was so clever that anyone known as "ty-wise" was much more intelligent than another man.

• † •

The Binding of Fenrir is one of the few surviving events that displays Tyr's persona and characteristics. When Loki's supernatural children (whom he fathered in secrecy) outgrew their home, Oðinn was able to see them from his throne. He knew they were the children of Loki, so he sent Thor and Tyr to capture them and bring them into Ásgarðr. One of them was a wolf cub named Fenrir. One was a serpent named Jörmungandr, and the third of Loki's children was a girl named Hel. The gods had previously learnt from prophecies that these three siblings would bring great harm and unhappiness to them, so Oðinn and Tyr acted accordingly to prevent any further harm from coming to their family.

Oðinn assigned Hel to rule the realm of the dead, and he threw Jörmungandr into the ocean that surrounds Miðgarðr. But Fenrir was different. Fenrir was growing so quickly that his strength couldn't be measured; that terrified the gods. In the early days, Oðinn decided that Ásgarðr was too holy of a place to kill, so they chose to permanently bind Fenrir with fetters. They approached the giant wolf casually, firstly, to not aggravate Fenrir and also to not arouse any suspicions in his mind. The gods said they wanted to know how strong Fenrir truly was, and he was willing to be a part of their experiment because as a young individual, he was looking for any opportunity to impress the gods.

The first chain they tried was called Læding but Fenrir shattered it by kicking his legs. The second chain was called Droma; it was twice as strong as Læding but it still couldn't hold against Fenrir's strength. Fenrir broke every chain in their possession, so the gods sent Skirnir, Yngvi's servant, to Svartálfheimr, where he found some dwarves. The dwarves crafted a powerful cord called Gleipnir that was as soft as silk, as light as air and with a magic power that was most rare.

They made the fetter of things that do not exist, so they could not be broken. The dwarves began with the foot falls of a cat, then they used the beard of a woman, the roots of a mountain, the sinews of a bear, the breath of a fish and finally the spittle of a bird. These things made the cord Gleipnir.

The gods took Fenrir to the island Lyngvi, in the middle of the lake Amsvartnir. Fenrir sensed something was off when the gods challenged him with their flimsy ribbon, and he refused to be bound. The gods said,

"If you cannot manage to tear this band, then you will present no terror to the gods, and so we will free you."

Although Fenrir's scepticism remained, he agreed to be bound if one of the gods were to place their hand in his mouth as a trust mechanism, in case he couldn't escape. All the gods backed away, except Tyr. He knew there was no other way to contain the giant wolf unless someone stepped up; he was the one brave enough to satisfy Fenrir.

Tyr placed his right hand in between Fenrir's jaws, and the gods began to tie him down. They drew the end of the cord, which was called Gelgia, through the slab of rock known as Gjöll and fastened it to the boulder Thviti, which sunk deep into the ground. When Fenrir struggled, it only made the bonds tighter. Fenrir realized he had been betrayed, and he bit down; severing Tyr's right hand. When Fenrir howled in agony, they thrust a sword in his mouth with the hilt resting on his lower jaw and the point in his palate. The saliva that runs from his mouth, forms the river called Hope. In the end, as Snorri says, everybody laughed… except Tyr. His bitterness compounded and he is no longer considered a promoter of settlement between people.

• † •

At Ragnarök, Tyr will meet Garmr, the bloody dog of death, who guards the halls of Hel. With only his left hand to wield a sword, he will drive the blade into the heart of the dog and put it down, but from the battle, Tyr's flesh will be torn from the bone and the god of war will die too.

ᚺᛗᛁᛗᛉᚨᚠᚱ
Heimdallr
(Hemm-dall-er)

HAGALAZ

Heimdallr (unknown meaning) is the cheerful watchman of Ásgarðr whose teeth are made of pure gold, which led to the kenning of gold being called "mouth-count." Sometimes, he is called Hallinskidi and sometimes Gulltani (*gold-tooth*). It can also be assumed that he was known as 'Hagal' at one point or another considering the first rune of the second ættir. He stands tall on the rainbow bridge Bi-fröst, armed with a trenchant sword and his trumpet Gjallarhorn, waiting for the day that the Jötnar break through the outer wall. On that day, he will sound his mighty Gjallarhorn and call the Einherjar to battle. Heimdallr built himself a hall called Himinbjörg, which is located at one end of the Bi-fröst. The name translates roughly to "heaven hills" or "sky cliffs." Oðinn says it is a pleasant house where he happily drinks his good mead.

For the length of each day, Heimdallr will stand erect on the rainbow bridge Bi-fröst, made of fire, water and air. In the morning, the gods travel over the Bi-fröst on horseback to attend meetings at the foot of the world tree, Yggdrasil. According to Snorri, the horses of the Æsir are named as follows: Sleipnir, Glad, Gyllir, Glaer, Skeidbrimir, Silfrtopp, Sinir, Gils, Falhofnir and Lettfeti. The owners of each horse is never specified but Heimdallr's horse is named Gulltopp and Baldr's horse was burned on his ship at his funeral. To signal the comings and goings of the gods, Heimdallr blows a soft note. Every day, the gods meet at Yggdrasil but Thor will find his own way there. Not once did he pass over the rainbow bridge as he feared that his heavy tread would destroy it.

It is stated in the poem *Grimnismál*, St.29,

"Thor will wade four rivers every day- the ones called Kormt and Ormt, and the two rivers Kerlaug- when he goes to meetings at the tree Yggdrasil."

Heimdallr was born to nine mothers, which shouldn't be confused with the daughters of the sea Jötun couple, Ægir and Rán. Although it would make sense, the two groups are explicitly named separately. In *Voluspá en Skamma* St.35, it is stated that,

"Those nine giant women gave birth to the noble spearman at the edge of the world."

Following that, in St.37, it reads,

"His mothers were Gjalp and Greip, Eistla and Eyrgjafa, Ulfrun, Angreyja, Imth, Atla and Jàrnsaxa."

NOTE: Gjalp and Greip are daughters of the Jötun Geirroðr, of whom Thor kills, and Jàrnsaxa is the name of Magni's mother. Whether they are the same is unclear.

The earth gave Heimdallr strength to grow, as did the cold sea and the blood of the boar. Heimdallr requires less sleep than a bird and can see over one hundred miles by day or night. The watchman can hear the sound of wool growing on a sheep's back; he can hear the sound of grass growing and anything louder than that. In the poem *Thrymskviða*, St.15, Heimdallr is referred to as the handsomest of the gods and is able to tell the future like other Vanir. Therefore, it is difficult to describe exactly who or what Heimdallr is.

In the poem *Voluspá* St.27, a Völva says,

"I know where Heimdallr hid his ear, under the heaven-bright holy branches of Yggdrasil."

This could either mean that Heimdallr sacrificed his ear for a greater purpose, or it could be a reference to something that is entirely unknown to us.

• † •

Heimdallr has no direct spouses, but he is the father of "social classes" among humans. He disguised himself under the alias Rigr and impregnated three women of different standings of wealth. Each successive couple became the parents to the first child born into a social class of Norse society. As he progressed, the couples became younger and richer.

The first couple were named Ai and Edda (great grandfather and great grandmother). Rigr stayed with them and was given low-quality food. He slept between them for three nights, and nine months later, they gave birth to a boy named Thrall. He is described as having an ugly face, knobby knuckles and fat fingers. He met a woman named Thir, and she is described as having scarred feet, sunburnt arms and a hook nose. They birthed children whose names represent the characteristics and common jobs of slaves in Norse society.

The second couple were named Afi and Amma (grandfather and grandmother). Rigr stayed in their home for three nights, a much more privileged household. It was a place of tidiness and possessions. Rigr slept between them for three nights; after nine months, a child was born, and his name was Karl. He exercised middle-class jobs. He tamed cattle, built barns and made ploughs. He had red hair like Thor, which is representative of the fact that Thor is a middle-class man, who protects the working-class people of the world.

Karl married a lady named Snor, who wore a veil to their wedding, and they exchanged rings, making it a formal ceremony. Together, they had children of whom they taught and loved. Their sons and daughters had names that represented personal qualities and achievements that would be common for middle-class people.

The third couple were named Fadir and Modir. Rigr noticed straw on the ground and a ring to knock on the door. The couple answered, smiling and holding hands. Rigr found Fadir pursuing a noble activity; archery. He was stringing his bow and making arrow shafts. Modir was perfecting her appearance by smoothing out wrinkles in her long dress sleeve, putting on a blue blouse (a very expensive dye) and a headdress. She is described as having a neck whiter than driven snow (white is used to describe beauty in people, because they weren't required to work long hours in the sun). In the dining room, Rigr noticed a white cloth on the table. He was given servings of hot bread, meat and poultry with wine to drink. The three comfortably sat and spoke until late into the night.

Rigr lay between them for three nights, and nine months later, they bore a child named Jarl. His hair was blonde, his cheeks bright and his eyes were as cruel and clear as vipers (snake-like eyes is signified as a noble characteristic which is evident in the Saga of the Volsungs especially). He learnt noble skills like horse riding, how to use a sword and swimming. He became a warlord and was generous with his money. He married a woman named Erna, a soft fingered, white and wise woman. She wore a veil to their wedding, and together, they had a son named Konr Ungr (meaning 'King').

Konr Ungr would learn fate runes and life runes; he would learn spells to save lives, dull blades and calm storms. He would learn the language of birds, spells to put out fire and induce sleep (these are all spells known by Oðinn). Rigr was the one to teach him the runes but Konr tricked him into learning the runes better than Rigr. When Konr Ungr was practising his archery on birds, a bird told him that he was wasting his time, when he could be killing men instead. Then he could claim all the things that they possessed. He thought hard and took this advice; this was the birth of the war-loving, noble class Viking society.

• † •

At Ragnarök, Heimdallr will sound his mighty Gjallarhorn, which can be heard throughout all the nine realms, and call the Einherjar to battle. When the army of Ásgarðr reaches the Vigrið plain, Heimdallr will face off against Loki, and they will both die at the hands of each other. Their lifelong feud will come to an end.

ᛒᚱᚨᚷᛁ
Bragi
(B(r)a-gi)

Bragi is a white-bearded poet and peacemaker who plays a golden harp in Valhöll. Oðinn says Bragi is the greatest of poets, like Yggdrasil is the greatest of trees. Bragi has much wisdom and an eloquent command over language which he channels into creative mediums such as writing poetry and speaking publicly. Bragi's mission is directed toward advocating peace between the different races. He travels the realms and is welcomed wherever he visits, whether it be the halls of the Æsir, Vanir, Jötnar, Dvergr or Álfar. Because of Bragi, poetry is often called "brag," and anyone know as "brag" (chief), man or woman, has eloquence beyond others' capabilities.

As Bragi travelled, playing music from his harp, the sound caused the trees to bud and bloom; the grass gemmed with countless flowers, and this is where he met his wife, the cheerful guardian goddess, Iðunn. She carved runes into Bragi's tongue but it isn't clear as to which ones.

In the poem *Lokasenna*, Loki directly insults Bragi, but he doesn't want a fight. He offers Loki a sword, a horse and a ring to stop slandering the gods but Loki taunts him further by saying that Bragi wouldn't have any treasure to give, implying that Bragi would never have a sword because he doesn't fight and he would never have earnt a ring for faithful service in battle because he is such a coward. In St.14, Bragi then responds,

"If we were outside, and you had not come inside Ægir's hall, I would be holding your severed head. I'd pay you back that way for all your lies."

So, it is evident that Bragi is a man who wants peace for all but is not a coward, like Loki implies. Not much else is known of Bragi's exploits, except that he has children, although they are never mentioned outside of Lokasenna. Loki proceeds to taunt Bragi, but his wife Iðunn steps in and says,

"I beg you, Bragi, think of your children by blood and by adoption, and don't slander even Loki here in Ægir's hall."

ᛁᛞᚢᚾᛏ
Iðunn
(E-th-oon)

Iðunn is a cheerful goddess who possesses a sacred fruit that keeps its consumer youthful. She shares her sacred fruit with the gods to keep them young and energetic. The origin of the holy fruit is unknown but Iðunn is the only one in all the cosmos to possess them. Her magic casket always produces more fruits, regardless of how many she draws out. She is a beautiful goddess and is sought after by many Jötun men for her playful charm.

Few stories involving the goddess Iðunn have survived the waves of time but one has surfaced in the Prose Edda. It begins with Oðinn, Loki and Hœnir travelling through Jǫtunheimr, where they found a herd of oxen and killed one to feed themselves. They set down for camp underneath a tree and attempted to cook the ox in an earth oven. When they checked the meat, it appeared not to have cooked. And when they checked again, it still refused to cook. Then they heard a voice above them and saw a large eagle perched in the tree there.

The Jötun named Thjazi was disguised as an eagle, using magic to prevent the ox from cooking. He said he would allow the meat to cook if he was given his fill. The gods agreed to the harmless request but Thjazi ate significantly more than they liked. Out of frustration, Loki grabbed a massive branch and used all his strength to hit the eagle but Thjazi saw it coming and used magic to stick the pole to his feathers. He pulled Loki in the air but stayed low to the ground. Loki's feet were dragged along the ground, smacking into stones, gravel and trees. When his arms were about to come free from the sockets, he vowed solemnly to what Thjazi wanted.

Thjazi said he would allow Loki to live if he was able to get Iðunn outside the walls of Ásgarðr. Oðinn, Loki and Hœnir travelled back to Ásgarðr and went about their business. The next day, Loki approached Iðunn and told her that he saw some beautiful golden apples, much better than her fruit, just outside the walls of Ásgarðr. She gullibly believed Loki and they travelled out into the forest, right to where Thjazi was waiting. Thjazi swooped down and flew away with Iðunn and her fruits of youth.

None of the gods were too concerned because they thought she went travelling with Bragi but once they began to age rapidly, they became alarmed and began to search for the missing goddess. Oðinn's back was getting weak and Thor couldn't lift the things he used to, so upon close investigation, it was revealed that she was last seen in Loki's company. When Oðinn called upon Loki, he admitted to what he did, and they forced Loki to get Iðunn back. He borrowed Freyja's falcon suit and flew to Jǫtunheimr. When he reached the hall of Thjazi, Thrymheim, he saw that Iðunn was home alone and Thjazi was out fishing. He swooped down and secured Iðunn in his claws after turning her into a hazelnut.

Loki raced back to Ásgarðr but Thjazi was right behind them, creating a storm wind as he flew. Fortunately, the gods had prepared plenty of firewood, which they lit up as Loki flew over the wall. The flames grew to enormous heights with great speed and Thjazi flew straight into them, scorching his wings off. When he fell out of the sky, the gods beat him to death and celebrated Iðunn's return. Thor took the eyes of Thjazi and threw them into the sky so he could watch over his daughter, Skaði. In the poem *Harbarthsljoth*, St.19, Thor said,

"I killed Thjazi, the bold giant; I threw the eyes of that son of Allvaldi into the clear sky."

ᚱᛁᚲᛁ
Loki
(Loh-key)

Loki is pleasing and handsome in appearance but sly in character and he takes advantage of those who are unsuspecting. In many cases, Loki is helpful to the gods but he is equally harmful; either way, he is always saving his own skin. In their younger days, Oðinn and Loki "blended their blood" and swore an oath that no drink would be served to one without the other, which is why the gods tolerate Loki for so long and allow him to cause strife among them.

Loki is the son of an Ás mother and a Jötun father, which is very uncommon, as most women marry to an equal or higher social status. The hierarchy follows something similar to: Æsir-Vanir-Jötun (descending). Loki's mother is named Laufey (meaning "leaf island") and his father is Fárbauti (meaning "dangerous striker"). He possesses a great degree of knowledge in the art of cunning and he has tricks for every purpose. He is very deceptive and uses it to save himself countless times over.

Loki was first married to the giantess, Angrboda (meaning "sorrow offerer"), and together they bore three children. Firstly, the daughter named Hel who is made up of half a body of light and half a body of dark, decomposed flesh who now rules the realm of the dead, also called Hel. Second, the giant serpent who encircles Miðgarðr, Jörmungandr (meaning "big monster") and lastly, they produced the colossal wolf that terrifies the gods, Fenrir. The gods believed evil was to be expected of these three siblings, mostly because of their mother's nature and even more so due to their father's. It would seem that Angrboda is deceased, considering what Oðinn says in the poem, *Baldrs Draumar*. He uses magic to force a *dead* Völva back to life, and at the end of their conversation, Oðinn says, in St.14,

"You are neither a witch, nor a wise woman—no, you are the mother of three monsters."

Loki would disappear from Ásgarðr for extended periods of time, which led Oðinn to believe that his old friend was doing something devious. Loki fathered these three children with his wife in secrecy, until they outgrew their cave and Oðinn was able to see them from his throne, Hlidskjalf. Then he told Thor and Tyr of what he learned and asked them to get the supernatural children from Jǫtunheimr.

In the poem *Voluspá en Skamma* St.40, it is said,

"Loki fathered a wolf with Angrboda. He produced Sleipnir with Svaðilfóri. But there was one child worse than all the others of those born to Byleist's brother Loki."

This is a reference to how Loki ate the heart of an evil woman. He found it half-burned, on a linden tree. He ate its entirety, and from that point on, he was pregnant with an evil child. From that child, all troll women are descended. After Oðinn had Loki's mutant children kidnapped, Loki was more inclined to remain in Ásgarðr, where he married the Æsir goddess Sigyn. Together they had two children, Nari and Narvi.

• † •

When the gods needed a wall built around Ásgarðr, Loki found a builder of Jötun origin. For his service, he desired the sun, the moon and the goddess Freyja. The gods were reluctant to accept the terms but Loki persuaded them to. Loki also allowed the builder to have the assistance of his powerful stallion, Svaðilfóri. The builder was given three seasons (18 months) to complete the wall, which seemed like an impossible task, but his stallion Svaðilfóri was able to pull a dozen of the massive bricks at a time.

The gods watched as the builder worked, and they slowly felt their hope fade away. They realized he was going to complete the wall in time. On the final day, Freyja was furious. Because Loki allowed the builder to have the assistance of its horse, Freyja, along with a few of the others said that Loki would deserve an evil death if he did not find a scheme in which the builder would forfeit the payment. Assuming that Thor was one of those, Loki was terrified, so he swore oaths to do so.

Loki shapeshifted into a mare and waited amongst the trees for the workers. When the builder and his horse came back with the next lot of granite, Loki neighed seductively at Svaðilfóri, and "upon realising what horse this was," Svaðilfóri broke from his reigns and chased Loki around the forest. This is how the gods got a wall for free and how Loki became impregnated with Oðinn's eight-legged steed, Sleipnir.

When the Jötun spun into a furious rage, Thor paid the builder's wages with Mjölnir. He shattered that Jötun's skull and sent him straight down to Niflheimr. The gods all went to their judgement seats, and they deliberated upon what had happened; oaths were gone back on, pledged words and promises, all the solemn vows that passed between them.

• † •

The sacred treasures of the gods have a confusing origin. Confusing as to whether Loki planned it or not. It all started when Loki cut off Sif's long golden hair at the roots; according to Snorri, it was done for "til lævisi" (the sake of deception). Of course, following this, Thor apprehended Loki and threatened to break every bone in his body if he didn't get a new head of hair for his wife. Thor said he must go find some Svartálfar (dark elves), but Loki went to the Dvergr (dwarves), which indicates that dark elves and dwarves are in fact the same species, or at least live within the same realm.

Loki first went to the sons of Ivaldi, who produced a golden head of hair for Sif. They also made a massive ship that has fair wind wherever it sails and a sacred spear that never misses; because Loki said these treasures would be judged by the gods. After Loki was in possession of the three treasures, he went to the blacksmith-brothers, Brokkr ("badger") and Eitri ("poison"). He made a bet with Brokkr, proposing that his brother Eitri couldn't make three treasures better than the ones made by the sons of Ivaldi. Loki was so confident he wagered his head and Brokkr accepted the terms.

Brokkr was working the bellows and Eitri was working the forge. First, they made an impressive golden boar that was faster than any horse. This worried Loki, so he turned into a fly and attempted to distract Brokkr by biting him on the arm. Although, this had no effect. The brothers continued working on the next treasure, a golden arm ring. This time, Loki bit Brokkr on the neck but he was still left unphased. The third treasure they crafted was a heavy hammer. Now, Loki was really worried, so he positioned himself between the eyes of Brokkr and bit down so hard that blood squirted into his eyes. This caused Brokkr to miscalculate during a crucial part of the construction, causing the shaft of the hammer to come out shorter than planned.

Loki and the two families of dwarves brought the treasures to the gods to be judged and Sif tried on her new head of golden hair; she was very satisfied, as it grafted straight back onto her original hair. The spear and arm-ring were given to Oðinn, the ship and boar were given to Yngvi and the powerful hammer was given to Thor. The gods and goddess compared their treasures and discussed which ones they thought were superior. They came to the conclusion that Yngvi's boar, Oðinn's arm-ring and Thor's hammer were much better treasures than the others, so Brokkr and Eitri won the bet.

Loki offered for a wager to win his head back but Brokkr said there would be no chance of that. Loki said, "Catch me then," as he ran away using his magical shoes that allowed him to run over sea and sky. Brokkr told Thor to catch him and Thor did so. Because Loki was a liar and a fraud, Brokkr decided to sew Loki's lips shut instead of killing him. Brokkr grabbed Loki's head and attempted to cut his lips with his knife but he was unable to pierce Loki's skin.

Brokkr said, "It would be better if my brother Alr were here" (meaning "awl," the tool used to sew leather), and as he spoke the word, his brother was there, and Brokkr used his brother to sew Loki's lips shut with a thread called Vartari. When Loki opened his mouth, the thread split his lips and caused permanent scarring.

• † •

In the poem *Lokasenna*, many of the gods are feasting at Ægir's hall. Shining gold lit the hall and the beer served itself. Oðinn came to the feast with Frigg, as did Bragi and Iðunn. Tyr was there, bitter about losing his hand to Fenrir. Thor didn't come, as he was out east fighting Jötnar, but Sif was there. Viðar was there as well as Njörðr and Skaði. Yngvi and Freyja were there too, with Yngvi's servants Byggvir and Beyla. Many other gods and elves were present too.

Ægir had two great servants, Fimafeng and Eldir. It was a great place of peace, and all the gods praised how good Ægir's servants were. For reasons that aren't explained, Loki hates when servants are praised, so he killed Fimafeng. Everyone shook their shields and drove Loki out of the happy hall.

In the darkness, Loki met with Ægir's other servant, Eldir. They discussed how not one of the people inside was a friend of Loki. Then Loki said, in St.3,

"I will go in to Ægir's hall and see this feast. I will bring them slanders and rumours, and mix their mead with misery."

When Loki entered the room, it became silent. He wondered why those proud gods didn't have anything to say. Bragi announced that they didn't want to share an evening's worth of drinking with Loki. Loki lashed back with insults pertaining to the argument over Bragi being a coward. Put simply, he called all the goddesses whores, claiming that he slept with the lot of them and said Oðinn was a pervert for using "womanly-magic" while disguised among humans as a witch. He bragged about killing Baldr and he taunted Tyr by bringing up the fact that Fenrir bit his hand off, and he suggested that Tyr's wife had a son with Loki (this is the only reference of *her*).

When Loki reached the end of his speech, Sif handed Loki a drink and asked him not to slander the gods and goddesses anymore. He drained the horn and said,

"You would be unique, Sif, if you actually were wary and unwelcoming to other men. But I alone know how you were unfaithful to your husband Thor- and I was the one you slept with."

Everyone could hear mountains shaking. They knew Thor was coming. When he entered, he said,

"Silence, you sissy, or I'll let my hammer silence you instead. I'll knock your head off your shoulders, and then you'll be silent- and dead."

Loki knew that Thor meant his threats, so he left Ægir's hall. After this, Loki built a house with four doors so he could see in all directions. He slept there but hid in the Falls of Frananger, disguised as a salmon during the day. He pondered what type of device the gods might use to catch him, and he fashioned two strings together to create a net; thus, the first net was created.

When Loki saw the gods were a short distance away, he threw the net into the fire and hid between two rocks as a salmon. When the Æsir reached the house, Kvasir was first to notice what was burning in the fireplace, and they recreated the gadget, assuming it was a device to catch fish. They threw the net into the waterfall. Thor held one end, with the rest of the Æsir on the other. Loki was quite confident that they wouldn't find him between the two stones but as they dragged the net over him, they realized something living was there. They went back over a second time, and then Loki swam to the front of the net and slipped into the waterfall. This time the Æsir saw where he went, so they went in two groups, and Thor waded along the middle of the river. In this situation, Loki saw two alternatives: swim out to the ocean or attempt to jump over the net, and this is what he did. When he jumped, Thor swiftly got his hand round fish-Loki but slid to the tail, and this is the reason the salmon's tail is tapered toward the end.

They took Loki deep below the surface, where his sons Nari and Narvi were. Then Oðinn turned Loki's sons into wolves and forced them to fight. The intestines of the slain son were then used to bind Loki to three sharp rocks, and then they turned to iron. Skaði took a poisonous snake and tied it over Loki, so the poison would perpetually drip onto his face. Sigyn, Loki's wife, sat there holding a bucket over him to catch the poison but when the bucket filled, she had to empty it and the poison dripped onto Loki's face again. When he trembled from the pain, the world followed, resulting in an earthquake on the surface. The bonds, made of his own son, will hold Loki until Ragnarök. After which, he will escape and lead an army of Jötnar against the gods.

• † •

At Ragnarök, a rooster will crow in each of the main worlds; in Ásgarðr, Gullinkambi will make the call; in Jǫtunheimr, a bright red rooster named Fjalarr will sing in Birdwood; and in Niflheimr, a soot red rooster will call in the halls of Hel. Fimbulvetr will fall upon the realms, three consecutive, terrible winters, and it will hit Miðgarðr the worst, as it states in *Voluspa* St.44,

"Brothers will fight one another and kill one another, cousins will break peace with one another, the world will be a hard place to live in. it will be an age of adultery, an age of the axe, an age of the sword, an age of storms, and age of

wolves, shields will be cloven. Before the world sinks into the sea, there will be no man left who is true to another."

Garmr will break from its chains at the Gnipa Cave and the sun will turn black. The earth will tremble as Loki breaks from his chains, and Heimdallr will sound his mighty horn. The ship Naglfar ("nail-ship," assumedly fingernail) will be loosed from its moorings, loaded with an army of Jötnar and dead soldiers and captained by the one named Loki. The surging tides will carry the ship to the Vigriðr plain, where they will meet Surtr and wage war against the gods.

Yggdrasil will sigh when the giant shakes it; she still stands but trembles. The Miðgarðsormr will move quickly through the waves in a monstrous rage, corrupting the sky and sea with poison. Oðinn will consult Mimir on behalf of the Æsir for a final time, and Fenrir will finally break its bonds as he howls terribly, storming toward the massive valley with its upper jaw in the sky and its lower jaw in the dirt; it would gape wider if there were room. The skies will divide as the sons of Muspel ride down on that valley.

Jǫtunheimr is roaring while the Æsir are in council, and the dwarves tremble at their doors of stone. Some call it Vigriðr, some Óskópnir and others Óskapt; nonetheless, this valley was chosen as it spans one hundred leagues in each direction. Surtr will come from the south with his massive sword made of fire that reflects the light of the sun. Yngvi will be without his good sword, but there will be a harsh conflict before he falls.

Oðinn will face Fenrir and be swallowed entirely, but his son Viðar will come screaming toward the wolf with his heavy shoe. His shoe collected all the leather scraps thrown away by men, which he will use to hold Fenrir's jaw open and drive the blade down its throat. When Oðinn is swallowed, that will be Frigg's second sorrow. Tyr and Garmr will eliminate each other, as will Heimdallr and Loki. The gods will meet their judgement, and the earth will sink into the sea. The stars will fall out of the sky, and Surtr will scorch the leaves of Yggdrasil, creating a bonfire that reaches the clouds, destroying the nine realms.

ᚢᛚᛦ
Ull
(Oo-ler)

Ullr is the son of Sif, yet his father is never named, which makes him the stepson of the thunder god, Thor. Snorri says he is a very handsome man with good combat skills. Ullr is an expert when it comes to archery and skiing; he is so good that no one can compete with him. Snorri refers to Ullr with many kennings, such as "snow-shoe god," "bow god," "hunting god" and "shield god."

From the kennings provided, it would be fit to assume that Ullr spends a great deal of his time in the snowy mountains, hunting and skiing. The kennings "ship of Ullr" is also used by Snorri, which could refer to the act of riding a shield down a mountainside or across an open ocean.

Ullr built himself a pleasant hall called Ydalir, which means "yew-dales." This would be representative of the fact that bows and snow-shoes were primarily made of yew timber in that time. In the poem *Grimnismál*, Oðinn is being tortured by king Geirröth between two fires. Oðinn says in St.42,

"Whoever first puts out the fire will have the help of Ull and all the gods."

Ullr was clearly a very important god at one point; this is also evident from the number of places that are named after the god Ullr, in Scandinavia.

In the poem *Atlakvitha*, St.31, it states that the hero Attila swore an oath by Oðinn's hill and by the ring of Ull on the day he was married to Guthrun. It is also mentioned by Snorri that it is good to call upon Ullr in duels. This could mean that Ullr has some presiding power over oaths and or the victor of single combat.

ᚠᚩᚱᛋᛖᛏᛁ
Forseti
(For-set-e)

Forseti is the keeper of justice in Ásgarðr, and all accept his judgement. He is the son of Baldr and Nanna and is described as being a radiant man. His hall is called Glitnir; it is made of golden pillars and a silver roof. This is the place where the Thing is held, and it is where disputes are settled among the gods. Forseti brings legal matters to a close and no one leaves his hall feeling cheated or unsatisfied with his decision.

Not much else is known from the Old Norse sources, but a legend is told of a divine intervention made by a man named Fosite. Forseti was heavily worshipped in Frisia, which is now known as a large part of the Netherlands. The Frankish King Charles Martel forcefully brought Christianity to a group of Frisian law-speakers. There were twelve of them, and they were considered high-ranking among their people. The Frankish king said they must submit to Christianity or fall victim to one of the following: execution, enslavement or be cast out to the open ocean without oars.

The law-speakers chose to be cast out to sea and prayed to the gods for help. It is then told that a thirteenth man appeared on the boat with a gleaming golden axe. Using the treasure, he steered the boat to shore. He then used it to chop into the land and bring forth a fresh-water spring. He said his name was Fosite, and he taught them a new code of laws and legal negotiation skills. The site of the fountain became a sacred shrine, but Christian writers replaced Fosite with Saint Willebrord.

ᛗᛁᛗᛁᛦ
Mimir
(Me-mere)

Mimir is a very wise god who lived among the Æsir for many years. In the poem *Hávamál* St.140, Oðinn says,

"I learned nine spells from the famous son of Bolthorn, the father of Bestla."

This has led scholars to believe that Mimir is the unknown brother of Bestla and therefore an uncle of Oðinn, but it is never explicitly stated.

Mimir was once a full-bodied man, but his head was removed after the Æsir-Vanir war. Two hostages from Ásgarðr were sent to Vanaheimr and three hostages from Vanaheimr to Ásgarðr. To solidify the peace treaty, the Æsir received Njörðr, Yngvi and Freyja. The Vanir received Hœnir and Mimir, which they thought was an excellent trade because of Mimir's wisdom and Hœnir's bold appearance.

The Vanir were happy with the trade until they realized that Hœnir was intellectually incapable of making a decision without first discussing with Mimir. The Vanir felt cheated, so in retaliation, they cut off Mimir's head and sent it to the Æsir.

Once Oðinn was in possession of Mimir's severed head, he smeared herbs over it so it would not rot. He spoke magic spells and gave it the power to converse with him. Oðinn didn't want such a wise man to go to waste; he wanted to extract every last piece of knowledge that Mimir had to offer. In doing so, he learnt many secrets.

Once Oðinn was satisfied with what Mimir had taught him, he set Mimir down at the well, Mimisbrunnr, which can be located under the second root of Yggdrasil, in Jǫtunheimr. Mimir would drink from this well daily to expand his already vast knowledge. Oðinn visited Mimir later and sacrificed his eye to the beheaded god for a drink of the wisdom-giving waters.

ᚺᛟᛏᛁᚱ
Hœnir
(Hoo-near)

Hœnir is a god who is mentioned very infrequently, and the given descriptions provided by our surviving sources don't seem to add up. Hœnir is mentioned as a travelling companion with Oðinn and Loki, but he is also mentioned in the poem *Voluspá* as the one to give souls to humans. This contradicts what Snorri tells us of the hostage exchange made by the Æsir and Vanir.

Snorri describes Hœnir as being swift and long-legged, alongside being handsome and a great warrior. His skills and menacing appearance are easily recognized, so when he was traded as a hostage to the Vanir, they immediately made him a chieftain. This position suited him well, until big decisions came his way. He couldn't come up with a conclusive answer and would always require the consolidation of Mimir. He would simply answer with, "Let others decide." The Vanir thought they had been cheated out of the deal, which resulted in Mimir's head being removed and sent to the Æsir.

• † •

At one point, Oðinn wanted to explore the whole world, so he brought Loki and Hœnir on his expedition. They came to a river and followed it to a waterfall, where they saw an otter who had caught a salmon. The otter was eating with its eyes half-closed, so Loki picked up a stone and hit the otter in the head. Loki was triumphant at his catch, as he caught an otter and a salmon in one blow. They took both the catches on their journey and found themselves at a farm, which they entered at their own desire.

The farmer was called Hreidmar; he was a person of great power and was skilled in magic. The Æsir asked for a night's worth of lodging, as they had plenty of provisions to share. The gods showed their catch, and when Hreidmar saw the otter, he called his sons Fafnir and Regin to see that their brother Ottar had been killed. They took the gods prisoner and bound them. The Æsir offered a ransom for their lives, as much as Hreidmar saw fit. These terms were agreed upon and confirmed with oaths. Hreidmar skinned his son and announced that the gods were to fill the skin with gold and cover it entirely.

Oðinn sent Loki to Svartálfheimr, where he came across a dwarf named Andvari. He was disguised as a fish in a lake but Loki caught him. Loki made Andvari get all his gold from his cave, which was a substantial amount. The dwarf slipped a small gold ring under his arm, hoping to savour it, but Loki saw it and told him to hand it over. The dwarf begged Loki not to take it, saying it could multiply his wealth if he kept it. Loki said he would not keep a penny's worth and took the ring. Andvari then pronounced that the ring should be the deadly destruction of whoever possessed it. Loki exclaimed that he was happy for that to be so, and Loki said the pronouncement would remain valid.

When Loki returned to Hreidmar's, he showed the gold to Oðinn, and Oðinn removed the ring from the treasure and began paying Hreidmar. Oðinn filled the otter skin and stood it up, and then he began covering the outside. When Hreidmar examined the skin, he saw a whisker poking out and said it must be covered; otherwise, it would mean the end of the agreement. Oðinn drew out the ring and covered the whisker, declaring that they were now free of the otter payment.

When Oðinn had taken his spear and Loki his shoes, they had no need to fear, so Loki pronounced that the gold should be the death of him who possessed it, which was subsequently fulfilled.

• † •

In the poem *Voluspá*, St.61, it states,

"Then Hœnir will speak forth his prophecies, and the two sons of Oðinn, the two brothers, will inhabit the heavens."

This would mean that Hœnir's is fated to survive Ragnarök, but his prophecies are never described in any further detail.

ᚷᛖᚠᛋᛟᚾ
Gefjon
(Gev-yune)

Gefjon is one of the primary members of the Ásyniur and appears to be a positive spirit who doesn't want any feuds between the gods. She speaks in *Lokasenna* and tries to calm the situation in St.19,

"Why should two gods exchange insulting words here inside this hall? I think Loki is a cheerful fellow; everybody loves him."

But Loki ridicules her for this and says in St.20,

"Silence Gefjon. I remember that boy who seduced you. That handsome boy gave you a necklace and you opened your thighs for him."

In the following stanza, Oðinn responds,

"You're mad, Loki, out of your wits, if you want to make Gefjon angry. I think she foresees the fates of all living things as well as I do."

• † •

In Gylfaginning of Snorri's Prose Edda, or "the tricking of Gylfi," begins with Gefjon and her sexual relation to the Danish King Gylfi. Snorri says that for the effort of Gefjon's entertainment, King Gylfi rewarded her with a hefty chunk of land, as much as four oxen could plough over a day and a night. She took four oxen from the North, from Jǫtunheimr, her sons and a certain giant. They drove the plough hard, so much that it uprooted the land and the oxen pulled the chunk of land out to the sea. To the west of Denmark lies the island known as Zealand, and Gefjon positioned it exactly where she wanted. According to Snorri, the place where the land was lifted left a lake which is known as Lake Mälaren in Sweden.

ᛈᚠᚱ
Vár
(Vo(r))

Vár is briefly mentioned by Snorri; he says that Vár listens to people's private oaths to each other and punishes those who break them. He also speaks of a goddess named Vor who can be assumed to be an extension of the other goddesses due to the nature of Snorri trying to create a "perfect" hierarchical structure. Vár, however, can be confirmed as a real goddess considering that she is also mentioned in the Poetic Edda by the king of giants, Thrym, at his wedding in the poem *Thrymskvitha*. He says in St.30,

"May Vár, goddess of wedding vows, bless us."

Therefore, it can be confirmed that Vár has some authority over marital practices.

ᚹᚢᛚᚠ
Fulla
(Fool-ah)

The goddess Fulla is a handmaiden of Frigg who wears a golden band around her head to control her beautifully free-flowing hair. Snorri says that Fulla is a virgin who carries the casket of Frigg and looks after her footwear. Snorri also says that Fulla shares many secrets with the queen of the Æsir, which would explain why she is impersonated by Loki in the poem *Baldrs Draumar*. Loki disguised himself as Fulla to trick Frigg into telling him that mistletoe did not swear an oath to protect Baldr, which resulted in Baldr's death. So, it can be concluded that Fulla has a relatively close relation to Frigg.

VANIR

ᚷᚢᛚᚠᛖᛁᚷ
Gullveig
(Gool-veg)

Gullveig (meaning "gold-drink") was a member of the Vanir tribe who practiced war-magic; a sorceress who could see the future. They say she knew magic; she knew witchcraft. She was the pride of an evil family. She came to Ásgarðr under the name Heith and spoke many prophecies of war.

The Volva who narrates Voluspa, says in St.21,

"I remember the first murder ever in the world, when Gullveig was pierced with spears and burned in Odin's hall. They burned her three times; often killed-not a few times! - she still would live again."

The gods went to their judgement seats and pondered whether they should endure Gullveig's depredations, suffer a loss or take action against them and get repayment for the harm that had been done. The Æsir decided to act against the people who sent the sorceress to them. Oðinn let his spear fly and that is what started the first war in the world. The Vanir knew war-magic and the outer wall of Ásgarðr was broken. The tribes fought for many years until it was decided that neither could beat the other and they made a peace treaty. An exchange of hostages resulted in peace between the realms. The Vanir gave Njörðr, Yngvi and Freyja and the Æsir gave Mimir and Hœnir.

ᚾᛃᛟᚱᛞ
Njörðr
(N-yor-th-er)

Njörðr is a very wealthy seafarer and fisherman who belongs to the Vanir tribe of gods. He became a great friend of Oðinn since he was brought to Ásgarðr for a hostage exchange, to ensure the peace treaty between the Æsir and the Vanir held. Njörðr has two children named Yngvi (more commonly known by his title, Freyr) and Freyja who came with him to Ásgarðr. The mother of his children is commonly believed to be his sister, Njörun or Nerthus. Incest and marriage between siblings was a common practice among the Vanir but certainly not the Æsir. Although, this doesn't deter Oðinn, he describes Njörðr in *Grimnismál*. St.16,

"The eleventh hall is Njördr's, which he built and named Noatun. That flawless lord of men rules that high-timbered place."

His hall is located at the ocean's edge, where he will spend much of his day, hunting sea creatures. Those who contact Njörðr with a strong desire are often granted land or possessions in return. According to the wise Jötun, Riddle-Weaver, Njörðr will be one of the few gods who survive Ragnarök. In Vafthruthnismál St.39, he states,

"Wise Vanir created him in Vanaheimr, and gave him as a hostage to the Æsir. At Ragnarök he will go back home to the wise Vanir."

After living in Ásgarðr for some time, Njörðr is eventually married to the giantess Skaði. This happened when Skaði's father, Thjazi, was killed by the gods for kidnapping Iðunn. She came to Ásgarðr, prepared for a fight but the gods decided to compensate her with something else. They said she could take one of the gods as a husband, under the condition that she made her decision based on the appearance of the gods' feet.

All the gods lined up behind a curtain, so only their ankles were exposed. Skaði peered carefully at the wide range of feet. She stared for a long time and chose the most beautiful feet, hoping they would belong to Oðinn's son, Baldr. But in fact, the most beautiful feet belonged to Njörðr, as they were so clean from wading through the ocean.

Njörðr and Skaði were happy together, but problems arose with their living arrangements. Skaði spent nine nights staying in Noatun, but she couldn't tolerate the seagulls squawking, as they woke her too early in the morning. In turn, Njörðr tried to live in Skaði's hall, Thrymheim, for nine nights, but he couldn't stay there because the wolves kept him restless at night. This resulted in them living separately in their own halls but still remaining in a relatively faithful relationship.

ᚼ᚜ᚠᛈᛁ
Skaði
(Skah-the)

Skaði is the daughter of the Jötun Thjazi, who was killed by the gods for kidnapping Iðunn. She inherited her father's hall, Thrymheim, which can be found in the snowy mountains of Jǫtunheimr. Due to her living conditions from a young age, she became very skilled at hunting and skiing. She has confidence and won't back down when threats come her way. She can be called the "ski-deity" or "ski-lady" and is known by the Æsir as the "bright bride of the gods."

Ever since her father was killed, she has sought out revenge against the gods. She came to the walls of Ásgarðr, armoured and ready to fight but the Æsir said they would compensate her in some other way: with a husband and laughter. She accepted the terms, and the gods lined up behind a curtain, with only their ankles exposed. She chose the most beautiful feet, which belonged to Njörðr.

Because Loki was responsible for Iðunn being kidnapped (and therefore Skaði's father being killed), Loki was given the responsibility of the other task; making Skaði laugh. He took one end of a rope and tied it to a goat's beard; he then tied the other end to his own testicles. He played tug-of-war with the goat until he fell into Skaði's lap, squawking in pain.

Now Skaði was a Vanir by marriage and widely accepted by all the gods. Skaði referred to Yngvi and Freyja as "our children," even though she was only their stepmother. Skaði is now a great friend of the gods and is included in many of their social gatherings and feasts. Skaði was at Ægir's hall in Lokasenna, when Loki insulted all the gods, and she was the one to place the venomous snake above Loki when he was captured and tied down. This could be an indication as to why her name translates to "injury," or it may be a trait found in beings of Jötun descent that their names have some kind of negative connotation.

ᛁᚦᛈᛁ
Yngvi
(Ing-vee)

INGWAZ

Yngvi is a fair and respectful god who is known to bring good season. To those who contact him with a powerful desire, he will respond with rain and sunshine, prosperity and peace. As the son of Njörðr, Yngvi was brought to Ásgarðr as a hostage to solidify the peace treaty between the warring tribes. Yngvi was only a boy at this time, so Oðinn gave him a welcoming present: the realm Álfheimr. Yngvi is often called "lord of the Álfar," which is probably how he received the more familiar title "Freyr," which translates to "lord."

Yngvi possesses two sacred treasures crafted by the sons of Ivaldi, one of those being the ship Skidbladnir. It is a magnificent ship but not the biggest; Naglfar is the biggest. Even so, Yngvi's ship can carry all the Æsir with their weapons and war gear. It will have fair wind as soon as the sail is hoisted, and regardless of the countless mechanisms within the ship, it can be folded into a cloth and stored to his pocket. Yngvi also has a powerful golden boar which is named Gullinbursti. This boar is special; it never tires and has golden bristles that always light the way ahead. It can travel over sky and sea, faster than any horse. In part of the poem *Voluspá en Skamma*, Yngvi's twin sister Freyja is riding Gullinbursti. She says in St.7,

"Gullinbursti glows, that battle-swine which two crafty dwarves, Dain and Nabbi, made for me."

Yngvi once had a divine sword that fought by itself *"when possessed by a wise man,"* but he traded it for the woman he loved. Yngvi snuck into Oðinn's high seat Hlidskjalf, where everything within the Norse cosmos can be seen. He gazed over all the realms and when he looked to Jǫtunheimr, he saw a beautiful woman, the daughter of Gymir; her name was Gerð. When she lifted her arms to open the door, light was shed over sky and sea; all worlds were made bright because of her. Yngvi became love-sick at the sight of her and felt he had to marry this woman.

Skaði noticed that her stepson was looking gloomy, so she sent Yngvi's servant, Skirnir, to ask what the matter was. Yngvi said,

"That woman means more to me than any woman has ever meant to any young man."

Skirnir said,

"Give me a horse that will carry me through darkness and flame. And give me your sword that fights by itself against enemy giants."

Yngvi gave his sword to Skirnir and Skirnir rode away. Although Yngvi may have successfully wooed the woman of his dreams, he was left with only an antler to fight the Jötun Beli. He could've killed that giant with his fist, but he will be at an even greater disadvantage when the sons of Muspel wage war against the gods.

When Skirnir arrived, he saw fierce dogs chained up outside the fence that surrounded the hall where Gerð lived. Skirnir rode up to a herdsman and asked how he could get past to speak with Gerð. The herdsman said he would never speak a word with Gymir's daughter but when she heard the commotion outside, she asked Skirnir to come in for a drink of mead.

She questioned Skirnir of his origin, and he said he was no Álfar, nor Æsir, nor Vanir. Skirnir proposed that she marry Yngvi; he offered Iðunn's fruit of immortality, he offered Oðinn's sacred arm-ring, and still, she denied the request. She would not accept any payment, and she said she would never marry him. After many threats and curses were made by Skirnir, Gerð agreed to marry Yngvi but insisted that he must wait nine nights before they could meet. Gerð said they would meet at a grove named Barri, and there, Yngvi would enjoy Gerð's love.

At Ragnarök, Yngvi will meet the Muspel giant, Surtr, whose massive sword made of flame reflects the light of the sun. Surtr will scorch the ground approaching the heroic son of Njörðr. Because Yngvi traded his sacred sword, he was left with only an antler to fight; and he fell that day.

ᚠᚱᛗᛁᛋᚠ
Freyja
(Froy-yah)

FEHU

Freyja (meaning "lady") is second in line among the Ásyniur and can be very easily confused with the queen of the Æsir, Frigg, due to the strikingly similar qualities they both possess. This has led some scholars to believe that Frigg and Freyja were once the same goddess but split many centuries later, possibly due to the Christianisation of Scandinavia. Although this may be the case, they each exist separately in the Eddas and contribute as separate entities in the poem *Lokasenna*. Therefore, the common belief among modern Vikings is that they are separate, and I will treat them as such.

Freyja is a goddess originally belonging to the Vanir tribe but was brought to Ásgarðr as a child alongside her father Njörðr and twin brother, Yngvi. As the twins were only young, Oðinn paid special attention to them to ensure they felt a warm welcome. Oðinn gifted the realm Álfheimr to Yngvi, and he spoke deeply with Freyja about the secrets of Seiðr magic, which he then practiced for many years disguised as a witch among humans.

Freyja is the one who arranges seats in the dining area of Valhöll, Fólkvangr. As it says in the poem *Grimnismál* St.14,

"Freyja rules in the ninth land, Folkvang- that is where she arranges the seats. She chooses half the dead who die in battle, and Odin takes the other half."

Many and most have interpreted these words to mean that Freyja takes half the warriors to somewhere other than Valhöll, but that is not what it says. Considering the sheer size of Valhöll, it would make more sense to assume that Oðinn takes half the warriors to practice fighting and Freyja/Frigg takes the other half to a dining area where she arranges the seats and the warriors are able to feast, drink and relax. This would also explain as to how the hall *Sessrumnir* (meaning "seat-room") became the name of one of Freyja's halls.

Freyja is married to the man named Oðr, who is only mentioned briefly by Snorri and never mentioned in the Poetic Edda, which also leads scholars to believe that Oðr is Oðinn. Together, they bore the daughter Hnoss (meaning "treasure"). Much like Oðinn, Oðr is travelling constantly. When Oðr travels, Freyja weeps. As time passed, Freyja became lonely and travelled in search of her husband. Therefore, Freyja is known under many names, like Gefn, Mardoll, Horn and Syr. Her tears are made of red gold and land on the earth's surface as amber stones, which led to gold being referred to as "Freyja's weeping," or "Freyja's eyes."

Freyja has a sexual appetite that is much greater than any of the other goddesses and she isn't ashamed of it. In the poem Lokasenna, Loki accuses her of having slept with every god and elf in the room, including her own brother. In Voluspa en Skamma, the seeress claims that her hog is actually her lover, Ottar, in disguise and to acquire her famous necklace, Brisingamen, she spent a night with each of the four dwarves who crafted it. In the poem Voluspa en Skamma, the giantess Hyndla, says in St.47,

"You ran after Odin, you're always lustful, and you've slept with many others."

It is true that Freyja's beauty is unmatched but there are many other great qualities to her. Although, this isn't noticed by the other races of Jötnar or Dvergr, as they make many attempts to win Freyja as their bride. The Jötun who built the wall around Ásgarðr requested Freyja as his payment, along with the sun and moon and the Jötun Thrym, who stole Thor's hammer, requested Freyja as his bride in return for the powerful weapon.

• † •

Freyja possesses a mantle of falcon feathers which she occasionally uses to search for her husband but Loki uses it much more frequently to travel into Jǫtunheimr, running errands for the gods. Freyja's primary mode of transport is her chariot, which is pulled by a team of skogkatts—a breed of felines of a similar size to lynxes.

Out of all the deities, according to Snorri, Freyja is the most approachable for humans to make contact with. She will help in love affairs and other matters of the heart. Freyja is very fond of love songs, which is interesting considering that under early Icelandic law code, love poems were illegal, and the penalty for composing a love poem would be lifelong banishment.

Grágás I, Laws of Early Iceland-

"If a man composes a love poem about a woman, then the penalty is full outlawry."

It is never explained as to exactly why this was the case, but it can be inferred that it was due to the proper order of marriage in early Iceland. The father of a woman had the final say as to whom his daughter was married to; therefore, if a poem was written and the woman then fell in love with that poet, it would be equivalent to courting the woman without the father's consent.

Freyja has a beautiful necklace known as the Brisingamen, which enhances her already impeccable beauty. When she was strolling through the realms, she saw four dwarves inside a stone, working on a golden necklace. She offered money and treasure for it, but they said they each wanted a night with her. She happily accepted the terms and four days later, she was one necklace richer. When Oðinn laid eyes on the necklace, he had an intense desire for it, so he told Loki to go get it for him. Freyja was sleeping in her house, which no man can enter, so Loki shapeshifted into a fly to bypass the spell and found a draught where the wall met the roof.

Freyja was sleeping in a way that the clasp of the necklace was unreachable, so Loki turned into a flea and bit her so she would turn over. He then turned into himself, unclasped the necklace and brought it to Oðinn. After which, Oðinn made various demands of Freyja in order for her to get it back. This necklace was apparently fought over by Loki and Heimdallr in the form of seals but unfortunately, that poem is lost. Snorri references it in his Prose Edda and says that when Heimdallr visited Vagasker and Singastein, he contended Loki for Brisingamen, but nothing else is known.

JǪTNAR

ᚠᚷᛁᚱ
Ægir
(A-gear)

Ægir and Rán are great friends of the Æsir, but they are of Jötun decent. The common belief of these two Jötun are that they are the personifications of the working elements of the sea. Ægir (meaning "ocean") is also called Gymir (meaning "engulfer") and Hler (meaning "roarer"). Rán (meaning "robber") is the more sinister aspect, as Snorri mentions she uses a net to catch those who travel at sea; whether those she catches are dead or alive is unclear. Ægir first travelled to the realm of the Æsir voluntarily, and although he was very skilled in magic, the gods were aware of his movements before he reached them, so they prepared a great welcome, although many things had deceptive appearances. In the evening, Oðinn had swords brought into the hall, which were so bright that light shone from them and no fire was necessary.

Three months after Ægir visited the gods, he invited them to his hall, which Snorri says is located on an island called Hlésey, which is now known as the Danish island Læsø; this is the largest island between Denmark and Sweden. Ægir and Rán host many great feasts and parties in their magnificent hall, which has glowing gold that illuminates the entire place like fire. Gold is called "Ægir's fire" for this reason.

Together they have nine daughters whose names all have a brief association with the characteristics and behaviour of waves. Ægir will often host parties in his hall and provide good hospitality for the gods. Ægir has many great servants who cook for and feed the gods when they visit.

In *Hymiskvitha*, Thor stared at Ægir fiercely and said, "You will often provide a feast for the gods," in an argumentative tone. Clearly, Thor was looking very menacing because this is all it took for Ægir to seek out some kind of revenge that could benefit them all. He sent Thor on a long mission to find a cauldron large enough to brew beer for all the gods.

Ægir hosted the party in which *Lokasenna* took place. Ægir had some great servants; they were so great that the gods gave praise to one of them, Fimafeng. For unexplained reasons, Loki didn't like a servant being the centre of attention, so he killed Fimafeng. The gods drove Loki out to the forest in anger, where Ægir's other servant, Eldir, met him. He attempted to help Loki and dissuade him from going back inside, but Loki was determined to mix the gods' mead with misery.

RF↑
Rán
((R)o-an)

Whenever Rán is discussed in Old Norse poetry, she is almost always discussed under the context of an unlucky seafarer being drowned and pulled down to an underwater abode. Considering Ægir's name means "ocean" and Rán means "robber," it seems that Rán drowns sailors and takes their possessions, but for what reason? This is never explained. In St. 18 of the poem Helgakviða Hjorvarðssonar, the hero Atli says,

"Witch, you have been here by the king's ships, you've waited in the fjord's mouth. You were meaning to give the king's men to Rán, if their spears didn't kill you first."

When Egill Skallagrimsson lost two sons at sea, he stated,

"Rán has much shaken me."

If you have made it to this point, I sincerely thank you and hope you are wiser than when you started. As you have probably already identified, the Norse Gods are different to other gods. They walk among us as equals and are only here to offer their strength and support in order for you to achieve your goals. But you must have the desire to become better for yourself and no other reason than wanting to become better, to gain their support. The catalysts you experience in life *are* pre-determined, although that doesn't mean your reaction and response is fated. It is up to your free will to make the best of a bad situation and learn. Balancing love and wisdom is the reason that your spirit has entered this life. By constantly seeking new learnings, you will accelerate your spiritual growth.

If you found value in this resource or enjoyed reading the content of this book, I encourage you to dive deeper on your path of self-discovery and self-improvement. On my website, you can find a list of educational resources about the Norse Gods and the Viking age to expand your knowledge in that regard.

What I learnt from writing this book, is that I am the one who dictates my success. Not Odin nor any other god, for it is my free will that decides how I will respond to the catalysts of my life. I am my own god. If you truly believe and accept this concept, your potential is limitless.

https://NeotericViking.com/resources

Thank you.

Glossary of Terms

Æsir- family of gods, Oðinn's family.

Álfar- race of beings that reside in *Álfheimr*. (light-elves).

Amsvartnir- lake where Fenrir was bound.

Andhrimnir- cook of Oðinn's hall, Valhalla.

Andlang – a dimension higher than that of the gods.

Andvari – Dverg who has his gold stolen by Loki.

Angrboda- deceased wife of Loki. Mother of Hel, Fenrir and Jörmungandr.

Ásgarðr - realm of the Æsir.

Ask - first male human.

Barri - grove where Yngvi married Gerð.

Baugi - brother of Suttangr, jötun.

Beli – jötun of whom is killed by Yngvi with a stag's antler.

Bergelmir - father of all Jötnar. Only surviving descendant of Ymir.

Bestla – mother of Oðinn.

Beyla - servant of Yngvi, wife of Byggvir.

Bi-fröst - rainbow bridge that connects Ásgarðr and Miðgarðr, guarded by Heimdallr.

Bodn – vat which holds the mead of poetry.

Bolthorn - Oðinn's grandfather, jötun.

Bolverkr - alias used by Oðinn, meaning '*evil-doer.*'

Bórr - father of Oðinn.

Breiðablik - hall of Baldr.

Brisingamen - necklace of Freyja.

Brokkr - dwarf blacksmith, brother of Eitri.

Byggvir - servant of Yngvi, husband of Beyla.

Draupnir - arm ring of Oðinn.

Droma - second chain used to bind Fenrir.

Drykkjumaðr - 'drinking-man.' Thor is the greatest.

Dverg (plural: Dvergr) - a race of short humanlike creatures that reside in Svartálfheimr. They are master craftsman who are descended from Ymir. They are turned to stone by sunlight and therefore live within stone and soil. (dwarf).

Einherjar - Oðinn's warriors who reside in Valhalla.

Eitri - dwarf blacksmith, brother of Brokkr.

Eldhrimnir - cauldron in Valhalla where pork simmers.

Eldir - servant of Ægir.

Elli - grandmother of Utgard-Loki, personification of old-age.

Embla - first female human.

Falls of Frananger - place Loki hid after killing Baldr.

Fárbauti - father of Loki.

Fenrir - monstrous wolf-child of Loki, enemy of the gods.

Fensalir - hall of Frigg.

Fimafeng - servant of Ægir who is killed by Loki.

Fjalarr - dwarf who kills Kvasir and creates Óðrerir.

Fólkvangr - the dining area of Valhalla, Freyja arranges the seats.

Freki - wolf of Odin, 'ravenous.'

Freyr - commonly used title for the god Yngvi.

Galarr - dwarf who kills Kvasir and creates Óðrerir.

Garmr - pet dog of Hel.

Geirroðr - jötun killed by Thor.

Gerð - wife of Yngvi, daughter of Gymir.

Geri - wolf of Oðinn, 'greedy.'

Gilling – a jötun killed by Fjalarr and Galarr and father of Suttangr.

Gimle - home of those who survive Ragnarök

Gjallarhorn - trumpet of Heimdallr.

Gjöll - rock used to hold Fenrir.

Gladsheim - land where the grove, Glasir is located.

Glasir - grove where the hall, Valhalla is located.

Gleipnir - final chain used to bind Fenrir.

Gnipa cave – entrance to Hel.

Golden-comb - rooster that wakes the Einherjar.

Griðr - mother of Viðar and friend of Thor.

Gullfaxi - horse of the jötun Hrungnir, gifted to Magni.

Gulltopp – horse of Heimdallr.

Gullveig- sorceress sent by Vanir to Ásgarðr.

Gungnir - sacred spear of Oðinn.

Gunnloð - daughter of Suttangr, lover of Oðinn.

Gylfaginning- beginning of time.

Gymir – another name for Ægir and the father of Gerð.

Hel - daughter of Loki and ruler of realm of the dead; also called Hel.

Hermöðr - hero sent to retrieve Baldr from Hel.

Himinbjörg - 'heaven hills' or 'sky cliffs', hall of Heimdallr.

Hlésey - island where Ægir's hall is located.

Hlidskjalf - Oðinn's throne that can see all the realms.

Hnitbjörg - mountain where Óðrerir was stored by Suttangr.

Hreidmar – father of Ottar, Fafnir and Regin. Threatened to kill the gods for killing his son.

Hrimthurs - old Norse term meaning 'frost-giant.'

Hrungnir - jötun killed by Thor.

Hugi - 'thought.'

Huginn - Odin's raven, 'thought.'

Hvergelmir - well where all rivers originate.

Hymir - jötun father of Tyr.

Hyrökkin - jötun who pushed Baldr's funeral pyre out to sea.

Jarngripr - iron gauntlets of Thor.

Járnsaxa - mother of Magni.

Jörð – personification of Earth, mother of Thor.

Jörmungandr – name for Loki's serpent son (meaning; big-monster).

Jötun (plural; Jötnar) - race of being who reside in Jǫtunheimr. Rival family of the Æsir and enemy of humans.

Jǫtunheimr - realm of Jötnar, east of Ásgarðr.

Kvasir - very wise god derived from communal spitting vat.

Læding - first chain used to bind Fenrir.

Læraðr - tree in courtyard of Valhalla.

Laufey - mother of Loki.

Litr – dwarf which Thor kills at Baldr's funeral

Logi - 'flame.'

Lyngvi - island where Fenrir was bound.

Magni - son of Thor.

Megingjörð - belt of strength worn by Thor.

Midgarðr - (middle enclosure), realm of humans.

Miðgarðsormr - son of Loki, also called Jörmungandr.

Mimisbrunnr - well of Mimir.

Mjölnir - hammer of Thor.

Modi - son of Thor.

Munin – raven of Oðinn.

Naglfar - 'nail-ship' sailed by Loki to wage war against the gods.

Nidavellir – modernized name for Svartálfheimr.

Niðhoggr – serpent which dwells beneath Yggdrasil.

Njörun - wife of Njördr and mother of Yngvi and Freyja.

Noatun - hall of Njördr.

Norns - the choosers of fate.

Oðr - husband of Freyja.

Óðrerir - the mead of poetry made from Kvasir's blood.

Ottar – son of Hreidmar, killed by Loki.

Ragnarök – fate or judgement of the gods.

Rati – drill used by Oðinn to bore the mountain Hnitbjörg.

Riddle-Weaver - jötun contested by Oðinn in mythological knowledge.

Rigr – alias used by Heimdallr while travelling through Miðgarðr.

Rindr - mother of Vali, jötun.

Roskva - child slave of Thor.

Sachrimnir - pig who's meat feeds Einherjar.

Seiðr - form of art used in making prophecies.

Sessrumnir - hall of Freyja.

Sigyn - wife of Loki.

Skidbladnir - ship of Yngvi.

Skirnir - servant of Yngvi.

Skrýmir - alias used by Utgard-Loki to trick Thor.

Skuld - a Norn (future).

Sleipnir - battle steed of Oðinn.

Snorri (source) - Christian poet who preserved pre-Christian beliefs.

Sodn – vat which holds the mead of poetry.

Sons of Ivaldi – Dvergr who crafted three treasures for the gods.

Surtr - jötun from Muspelheimr who wages war on the gods.

Suttangr - jötun who stored the mead of poetry in the mountain Hnitbjörg.

Svaðilfóri - father of Sleipnir.

Svartálfheimr - realm of the Dvergr (dark-elves).

Tanngnjostr - goat of Thor.

Tanngrisnir - goat of Thor.

Thing - place where legal matters are resolved.

Thjálfi - child slave of Thor.

Thjazi - father of Skaði.

Thokk - alias used by Loki to keep Baldr in Hel.

Thrud – daughter of Thor and Sif.

Thruðheim - realm of Thor.

Thrym - jötun who stole Thor's hammer.

Thrymheim - hall of Skaði.

Thviti - boulder that held Fenrir.

Urð - a Norn (past).

Utgard-Loki - jötun who deceives Thor and Loki.

Valaskjalf- the place where Hlidskjalf is located.

Valgrind – holy gate used to transport men's souls to Valhalla.

Valkyrie - maiden of Oðinn who reaps the souls of men.

Vanaheimr - realm of the Vanir.

Vanir - family of gods.

Ve – brother of Oðinn.

Verðandi - a Norn (present).

Vidblain – a dimension higher than Andlang which is only inhabited by beings of light.

Vigrið plain – the place where the gods will meet their fate.

Vili – brother of Oðinn.

Valhöll (Valhalla) – hall of Oðinn. Home of the Einherjar.

Volsungs – human family descended from Oðinn.

Volva - witch who makes prophecies.

Ydalir - hall of Ullr.

Yggdrasil - ash tree that connects the realms.

Ymir - first being to exist.

Sources

- The Poetic Edda translated by Dr. Jackson Crawford

-2015

- Edda by Snorri Sturluson translated by Anthony Faulks

-1995

- The Saga of the Volsungs translated by Dr. Jackson Crawford

-2017

- The Wanderer's Hávamál translated by Dr. Jackson Crawford

-2019

- Gods and Myths of Northern Europe by H. R. Ellis Davidson

-1964

- Njal's Saga translated by Leifur Eiriksson

-1997

- Dictionary of Northern Mythology by Rudolf Simek

-1993

- Ásatrú for Beginners by Mathias Nordvig PhD.

-2020

- Taking up the Runes by Diana Paxson

-2005

- Northern Mysteries & Magick by Freya Aswynn

-1998

Made in the USA
Coppell, TX
11 May 2021